HARMONY IN CHAOS

BARBARA FOXE

Harmony in Chaos

Ramakrishna Vedanta

RIDER

London Melbourne Sydney Auckland Johannesburg

Rider and Company

An imprint of the Hutchinson Publishing Group

3 Fitzroy Square, London WIP 6JD

Hutchinson Group (Australia) Pty Ltd
30–32 Cremorne Street, Richmond South, Victoria 3121
PO Box 151, Broadway, New South Wales 2007

Hutchinson Group (NZ) Ltd
32–34 View Road, PO Box 40–086, Glenfield, Auckland 10

Hutchinson Group (SA) (Pty) Ltd
PO Box 337, Bergvlei 2012, South Africa

First published 1980

© Barbara Foxe 1980

Set in Intertype Baskerville

Printed in Great Britain by The Anchor Press Ltd
and bound by Wm Brendon & Son Ltd
both of Tiptree, Essex

ISBN 0 09 142061 X

Dedicated to all who seek harmony in life and in themselves, especially to all members, monastic and lay, of the Ramakrishna Movement all over the world, and its friends, associates and well-wishers; in particular to the late Swami Ghanananda, founder of the Ramakrishna Vedanta Centre in the UK.

CONTENTS

AUTHOR'S NOTE

A Bibliography at the end of this book gives details of all books from which quotations or references have been taken. I feel that this may be more helpful to the reader, and less distracting, than the insertion of footnotes on individual pages throughout. The original words of the people concerned were recorded fully during their lifetimes or shortly afterwards, and published at that time, so there is no conflict of evidence which might have made footnotes necessary; I hope, therefore, that a full Bibliography will prove more useful to those who may wish to explore further.

Barbara Foxe

FOREWORD

The book *Harmony in Chaos* is a simple and lucid exposition of the lives and teachings of Sri Ramakrishna and his well-known disciple Swami Vivekananda, but it is not merely an intellectual thesis. The author, in the course of her long association with the Vedanta movement in the British Isles, has developed an insight into the Vedanta philosophy, as she has shown in her earlier book, *Long Journey Home*, an authentic life of Margaret Noble (Sister Nivedita). Barbara Foxe has been a close associate and good friend of the Vedanta movement; and in books, articles, and in her writings for radio she has also shown that she is well aware of the problems of life in the West today.

This book offers to the reader the basic facts about the lives of Sri Ramakrishna and Swami Vivekananda and, quoting extensively from their own words, gives their message in its application to the modern West. Today, more perhaps than in any other period, the West is keenly feeling the need for spirituality. Having lived, in recent decades, in much more widespread prosperity than his forefathers, modern man sometimes feels that he has lost sight of any worthwhile purpose for his life. It often seems to have become boring and meaningless, or even to lack deep value or a goal. Civilized life is in many ways chaotic; it lies in disarray.

Harmony in Chaos carries the message of harmony and universatility. It is necessary for us to harmonize the different aspects of life which we find within ourselves, and in the world around us; to bring harmony between the inner and contemplative life and the active life; between ourselves and other people with their different natures; between many different approaches to the Truth. We have to be individuals in our own highest potential and yet live in harmony with our society and with the world as it is. *Harmony in Chaos* throws light on these needs. Sri Ramakrishna and Swami Vivekananda were men of great spiritual achievements who lived amongst the hard facts of life. Their words and their lives bring a conviction of the divinity of man and of his spiritual foundation. Barbara Foxe shows us that their teachings were explicit and clear, but without either rigid dogma or a facile blurring of difficult issues; their words and their lives speak to people in all religions and to those who claim no orthodox religious belief.

I am sure that this book will stimulate the interest of readers and will send many to seek out the original sources for further spiritual enlightenment.

Swami Bhavyananda
President
The Ramakrishna Vedanta Centre
Bourne End, Buckinghamshire

He is indeed a real man who has harmonized everything.

RAMAKRISHNA

Amidst this chaos there is harmony, throughout these discordant sounds there is a note of concord; and he who is prepared to listen to it will catch the tone.

VIVEKANANDA

Symbol of the Ramakrishna Vedanta Movement showing the harmony of the four yogas in the nature of man. (See page 128 for full description.)

INTRODUCTION

'The swan has taken its flight to the lake beyond the mountains; why should it search for the pools and ditches any more?'

These are the words of Kabir. The question they ask echoes in the minds of those of us who are involved in life and its difficulties, and may at first arouse a response which is almost another question; the two words, 'Yes. But – ?'

In that response, sincerely spoken, lies the whole essence of our search.

The West sees the dangers of escapism, lethargy, or refusal to fight difficulties efficiently, as clearly as the East has always seen the dangers of attachment, over-anxiety, and the nervous tension which is destructive rather than creative. Both meet at the same point – a desire for the certainty of inner experience, not theory.

The greatest spiritual metaphors use as their illustrations, beauty which is fluid, translucent, or ever-changing; never static and unmoving. Water, light, music. And yet these things are never vague or weak. Water wears away a rock. Light comes though an ageless cosmic process, and the bringing of light to a dark room is the result of man's thought, invention, care, and often complicated hard work; the creation of music is one of the most highly disciplined of all arts, but when a symphony is played we hear something which flows as naturally as bird-song, and we recognize the pure note of simplicity. All bird-songs differ. So do symphonies. A world where only one bird sang and only one note of music sounded, would be a planet less chaotic perhaps, but certainly much more bleak than our own.

What, then, stands between the swan and its lake, casts a shadow across the light, and drowns out the sound of harmony? Saints and sages, gurus, teachers, philosophers and, above all, the great Incarnations, have all told us that it is man's own ego which creates an illusion of weakness, separation, and loss; that the kingdom of Heaven – the wholeness of peace, joy, and certainty – is within us. But when the reply has been given, we still stand where we did. What strength of character, what simplicity of grace is needed, to experience fully that great self which, though now only 'seen in a glass darkly', we already are?

We might even ask why, even in the darkest days, our sense of humour is so often a wiser guide than the prophets of doom.

The next words of Kabir's poem give us the meaning of the lake on which the swan sails. 'Your Lord dwells within you.' The word 'Lord', meaning 'the great one', may be taken by people with different philosophies, different religions or none, and certainly with greatly differing natures, in ways which at first seem various almost to the point of speaking many languages, or playing a different tune. And how *many* are the lakes?

One of the greatest gifts that Ramakrishna gave to the world was a full acceptance not only of all religions and all seeking, but of how greatly the inner natures of people do, in fact, differ. In them all he saw, not in theory but in full spiritual experience, the same light shining, whether clearly or dimly, and the same goal ahead. The goal is the experience of one's own complete identity, all that is meant by the words 'I am'. In all the yogas, in all true religions and philosophies, in the seeker who does not give any name to what he has found, and in those who can accept only the identity which the world sees, and doubt if they have any other – in all, the word 'Lord' represents identity in its finest sense. And if the Lord is within us, then He (or That) is within all. In the words of Krishna, in the *Bhagavad-Gita*, 'Who sees his Lord within every creature, deathlessly dwelling within the mortal, that man sees truly.'

But.

To attempt to catalogue the 'buts' would be presumptuous. Each one of us has his own list. The chaos we experience in the world in which we live is often expressed by sincere people who feel that they are living in an era where the guide-lines of morals and ethics, the certainties of religions and philosophies or even of outlook, are breaking down. The divisions between peoples, politicians, classes and power-blocks; the growth of violence, the over-emphasis on sexuality, the anxiety and tensions – the list is not a happy one. But it never was, in any Age. The media may seem to us to be obsessed with the alienation, fragmentation and conflict within Man's inner nature, without offering any healing or solution. At the other extreme of the spectrum, the Victorian era in Western countries tended to cover all such darkness with a heavy blanket of respectability and convention, while thousands of people who could not share such smug optimism, choked for air.

Intelligent and thoughtful people have never really needed to be told that this world, and their own natures, are not in every respect as they would wish. In *The Pickwick Papers*, a book for which Swami Vivekananda had a great affection, Sam Weller, much accustomed to poverty and the toughness of life, was cleaning the boots of visitors at a Victorian inn, when he was addressed with kindly condescension by a well-to-do visitor, who said : 'This is a curious old house of yours.'

He was expecting in reply, the grateful servility of the poor, but he did not get it. ' "If you'd sent word you was a-coming, we'd ha' had it repaired," replied the imperturbable Sam.'

As visitors on this planet, we may often feel that it might have been better repaired before we arrived; and yet a basic instinct tells us that here we are both at home and not at home; we reject in part, and yet in another way we feel a member of the family; we long for freedom and yet we dread loneliness and insecurity.

The cynics tell us that we might as well ask for hot ice.

Great souls have never been cynics. They took that basic certainty which is in all of us, and having found it in themselves, they went on to develop the spiritual faculty which most of us only glimpse, until all paradoxes were resolved. And always they combined detachment with love, meditation with compassion, and deep seriousness with lightness, humour and joy. Every one of them reached their heights in the darkness of the times in which they lived, and what they found, they shared. Their words were always explicit and without compromise, but cast-iron dogma, theory, or intellectualism were never a part of their equipment. These came at a later stage, in some cases, often centuries later, for it is then that sectarianism and a hardening into opposing camps, can bring a new form of chaos. History has never been without its great souls; some of them died unknown, others have influenced millions, but they all had one thing in common; they found in every one of us the same great potential that they had demonstrated in their own lives, however different the degree of manifestation. They were concerned with harmony, not with fame or power. They were givers.

Ramakrishna and Vivekananda lived in times sufficiently near to our own to seem very close to us, both through the records and writings of every kind, and in the lives of their disciples and those who knew them. Indeed, one Western disciple of Vivekananda, who became a monk of his Order, died as recently as 1966. Ramakrishna himself died in 1886, Vivekananda died in 1902. They lived in a period of history in which many of our present difficulties were recognizably beginning. When Vivekananda walked the length of India, after his Master's death, he saw suffering on a vast scale, physical and spiritual. Later, when he lived and taught for some time in England and America, he found a different suffering and a different lack. Like Ramakrishna, he refused to wear blinkers when he looked at life, or to avoid difficult questions.

The great humanitarian works of the Ramakrishna Movement are well known, because they can be seen by anyone who visits India today. Vivekananda founded the monastery, the Belur Math, at Calcutta, from which flows work of famine relief, hospitals, orphanages, education and much else for the poor and suffering, work and service given by both monastic and lay workers, as he said, from the heart in a spirit of love for God manifested in our fellow-men and in all nature. It is an expression of Karma Yoga, the yoga of dedicated work. In Western countries, he established Ramakrishna Vedanta Centres to foster the teaching of meditation and the living-out of spiritual harmony within the spirits and minds of people 'out in the world'. He wished to avoid organization as such. But practical humanitarian work requires some organization; Centres cannot be run without it; monks of the Order are still sent from India, as they were then, to act as spiritual advisers, and as gurus where this is required. But Vedanta has always insisted that yoga is a 'Do It Yourself' way of life, as we might say today. Ultimately, as Vivekananda said, the soul is its own teacher. Also he wished to include people of all religions, or of none; those who seek the Absolute as well as those who worship Ramakrishna as that same One who is also manifest in Jesus, Buddha, Krishna, and all other Incarnations of God, or perfected souls. The devotees of Ramakrishna all over the world today, can be numbered in millions, but worship of him or unquestioning obedience to any dogma has never been demanded as a ticket of admission. There must be no attempt to convert, he insisted . . . 'No name-and-fame making, no newspaper humbug,' as he said. 'Steady and silent work.' And so it has been, ever since.

In the West, the question is sometimes asked, 'Who was Rama-krishna? Is there a sect called Ramakrishnaism?' Vivekananda is known as one of India's national heroes, prior to Gandhi, but he himself, though he was loved as a great human figure as well as being revered as a yogi and teacher, always regarded himself as only the 'Saint Paul' whose task was to spread the great tide of spirituality of which Ramakrishna was the inner heart, the ever-present sustainer, even after his death.

Ramakrishna rejected utterly any personality cult which might possibly have arisen, based on himself. Such an idea was repugnant to him. On the essentials of his teaching and his spiritual experi-ence he stood adamant, and Vivekananda, also, stressed that in Vedanta all must be clear, never vague, indefinite, or facile. But there are many natures, many approaches. Ramakrishna said constantly, 'Truth is One. Men call It by many names.' He likened himself to a mother who gives all her children the same food, but cooked in different ways to suit their different needs, ages, or digestions. This, however, never implied a muddled eclecticism which jumbled together the easiest and most attractive portions of different religions and philosophies, and it went far beyond an ecumenical toleration, or a kindly acceptance of the warring elements within Man's nature, as we shall see.

The swan sails on its lake, as Kabir said – here and now. The loving and joyful life, the heights of spiritual experience, and the teachings of Ramakrishna, demonstrated that, as a fact, not a theory. In the symbol which Vivekananda chose to represent the harmony of the four great yogas in the psyche of Man, the swan represents the Great Soul – the Lord within, in the words of Kabir. And the swan sails on the waters of Karma – even when they seem to be very stormy waters. The seeker's 'Yes!' is the true, the instinctive response, but Ramakrishna also encouraged the 'But – ?' and answered it fully. For it is in this world that we live at the moment, and truth must stand the test of everyday living, or it is not Truth. We know that progress can only develop, for each one of us, from exactly where we stand now.

RAMAKRISHNA

On 16 August 1886 there died in Calcutta a man known as Ramakrishna. He left no property, because he owned nothing. He had established no sect in a world already full of sects, religions and philosophies, each proclaiming, 'Only *my* truth is Truth.' He gave no public lectures and would not accept or touch money. Some people regarded him as a great yogi, a prophet or a saint, some worshipped him as an Incarnation of God; but he brushed aside all attempts to place him on a pedestal, with the words, 'As long as I live, I learn,' in total rejection of any idea of cosily settling down in the spiritual stage one had reached, in order to enjoy the view. Indeed, when, in his youth, great pundits of the day decided, after much discussion, that this phenomenon called Ramakrishna was an Incarnation of God, he simply said that he was glad it was not a disease, and continued his pursuit of truth until he had reached a state of hard-won bliss which did not leave him even at the end of his life in the agony of a slow death by cancer, unrelieved by drugs.

Whatever Ramakrishna had found for himself, he gave away to others. Those seeking truth came to him because they were torn by chaos within, or by the difficulties and tragedies of life itself, and in him they found one whose whole mind, body and spirit had become totally absorbed in That which they were all seeking. He had discovered in fact, not in theory, that this experience could be reached through any one of the world's religions, and he also welcomed those who were sceptical of all the religious orthodoxies, but who were still seeking. Sincerity he regarded as the bedrock. His love, and his sense of humour and laughter as well as a certain childlike quality in him, overcame the awe that his spiritual state, his renunciation, and his strength of will might have aroused in those who came to him; and although he said that the words 'Guru', 'Master' and spiritual 'Father' pricked him like thorns, he became all these things to those who needed him, in varying degrees.

Although this life was lived out in apparent obscurity, today the Ramakrishna Order is the largest monastic order in India. Ramakrishna Vedanta Centres have spread across the world; in America and Europe the emphasis lies especially on the encouragement of meditation and the spiritual life; in India humanitarian work, also, is undertaken on a scale that takes several pages even to list. But it is sometimes forgotten when the observer sees that hundreds of thousands of people in India yearly receive famine relief, flood relief, nursing, maternity care, schools, colleges, libraries, agricultural training, and much more, that none of this proceeds from philanthropy or any desire for busy organization as such. A direct disciple of Ramakrishna once remarked quietly to a bombastic philanthropist who came to him, full of plans, 'I wonder what God did before you were born?' What is regarded as important is the attitude of mind and spirit; the reason *why* things are done. An equal part of the harmony is the life lived out in quiet devotion to domestic duty or to any vocation whatever which is truly one's own; the discovery of 'That' which is commonly called God, within us in meditation and the service of It in others; the harmony not only between the yogas but between all religions and approaches to God, and between the apparently opposing aspects of Man's restless nature and psyche. But to consider the teachings, we must first consider, however briefly, that life from which all this has flowed.

On 18 February 1836 a boy called Gadadhar, who was later known as Ramakrishna, was born in the village of Kamarpukur, seventy miles along the old road from Calcutta along which pilgrims and monks travelled to visit the famous shrine of Jagannath at Puri. The villagers were mostly farmers and craftsmen, and there was a simplicity in their daily lives which, without being idyllic, was almost centuries away from life in Calcutta, and further still from British and Western thinking in the universities of Bengal. The caste system was observed, but not in its more extreme and ugly forms; the women lived in the seclusion of purdah, but met in each other's houses and gossiped by the well when they fetched water; religious festivals and story-telling and singing were a part of the life of the community, and there was the constant interest of the pilgrims who passed through the village and stayed at the pilgrim house. Unlike many Indian villages, there was here no ill-will between the various religious sects of Hinduism. There was a degree of tolerance and acceptance which was by no means typical of the world outside, and Gadadhar grew up with one note of that harmony already a part of his thinking.

His father, Khudiram, was much respected in the village for his religious devotion and meditation, and also for his blazing honesty. He first came to Kamarpukur because he refused to give false evidence against a man who was being persecuted by the landlord of the village in which he previously lived. One of the less idyllic aspects of Indian village life was the total power of the landlord, who in this case promptly seized the whole of Khudiram's paternal property. A friend invited him to live in Kamarpukur, and gave him some of his own land and a few thatched huts for living quarters; here Gadadhar was born and grew up. Gadadhar's mother, Chandra, was simple, loving and totally guileless; everyone in trouble came to her. Her son described her as 'the personification of gentleness. People loved her for her open-heartedness.'

From a very early age, Gadadhar showed a strong will, a passion for truth which refused to be fobbed off by anything less, and a loving nature which greeted people, even on first meeting them, as though they were his oldest friends. He had a very strong sense of humour and fun, and on occasion he could be an imp of mischief. He was extremely popular in the village, especially as he had gifts of acting, mimicry, singing and story-telling; he could repeat by heart the great Hindu epics and mythology. It is not surprising that, in later years, he said of his childhood that he went from house to house 'like a happy pigeon'. He also began to develop a concentration so deep that it sometimes led to a loss of ordinary consciousness which alarmed his parents. He later described the first time this happened to him, when he was six or seven years old.

One morning I took parched rice in a small basket and was eating it while walking on the narrow balks of the cornfield. In one part of the sky there appeared a beautiful black cloud charged with rain. I was looking at it while eating the rice. Very soon the cloud covered almost the whole sky, when a flock of milk-white cranes flew against that black cloud. It looked so beautiful that I became very soon absorbed in an extraordinary mood. Such a state came on me that my external consciousness was lost. I fell down and the rice got scattered near the balk. People saw it and carried me home. This was the first time that I lost external consciousness in ecstasy.

He told his worried parents that though outwardly unconscious, he had experienced a bliss that was quite unlike illness, madness, or any kind of fainting fit. There were other similar occasions, including one when he was called on unexpectedly to act the part of the god Siva in a play, and his absorption in his role became so deep that he lost all external consciousness, and the play had to be stopped.

His determination and his loving nature were shown at the age of nine, when at his investiture with the sacred thread, an important ceremony in the life of a Brahmin boy, he insisted on keeping his promise to his old nurse Dhani; she wanted to feed him as a part of the ceremony, but this was reserved for someone of equal caste and Dhani was of the blacksmith caste. But Gadadhar would not break his promise; caste was put aside and Dhani had her wish. On another – more mischievous – occasion, when he was a youngster of thirteen, a rich man called Durgadas Pyne boasted that nobody, not even Gadadhar, whom he liked and trusted, had ever seen the women of *his* house, or the rooms in which they lived in strict purdah, and nobody ever would. It was a rash comment. Shortly afterwards, a poor weaver woman, heavily veiled, asked for shelter and was taken to the women's rooms, where 'she' spent the evening chatting politely with the women and only emerged when Gadadhar's brother arrived, asking anxiously if anybody had seen the boy, who for some reason could not be found. Mercifully, Durgadas had a sense of humour, and after that day the women of his family were allowed to join the other women of the village when they listened to the boy reciting the great epics, singing religious songs, or acting in plays.

Life was not always so happy, however. When Gadadhar was seven, his father died. It was a terrible blow to the little family, and a deep personal loss to the child. He drew closer to his mother, he gave more help in the house, and his inner questionings about the insecurity and transitoriness of life drew him to the pilgrim house, where he listened to the monks who sheltered there when they passed through the village. Their discussions about religion, their meditation, their detachment and serenity fascinated him; he also noted that some of them were hypocrites and scavengers who deceived themselves as well as others. He watched, he listened, he became more introspective.

Gadadhar's two elder brothers now struggled to support the

family. The eldest, Ramkumar, was left a widower when Gadadhar was thirteen, and his baby son, Akshay, was brought up by Chandra, helped by Gadadhar, who must have seen in his little nephew the eager, trusting child-nature which he so often described later as a vital part of spiritual progress. Years later, Gadadhar – then Ramakrishna – described how he had seen Akshay die, as a young man. He saw, in ecstasy, how Ashkay's soul was totally separate from the body and at the moment of death was withdrawn, like a sword from a sheath, leaving the body. 'I felt great joy to see it. I laughed and sang and danced.' But next day, when no longer in ecstasy, he realized that Akshay had gone from the world, and human grief seized him. 'I felt as if my heart was being wrung in the way a wet towel is wrung.' To those who came to him broken with grief by the death of a loved one, he told the story of Akshay and other deaths in his own life; and then from experience, not in cold-blooded theory, he reached their hearts and showed them, from his teachings, the way to face and overcome grief.

When Gadadhar was seventeen, Ramkumar, who was then teaching in Calcutta, sent for Gadadhar to help him. He also hoped to improve the boy's education; simple knowledge of reading and writing, which he had learned at the village school, plus a hatred of arithmetic, strong gifts for painting, singing, acting, story-telling, and a longing for the life of a monk, were not very hopeful assets for a career in Calcutta.

It was the boy's first experience of the city, and the difference between Kamarpukur and Calcutta was a great deal more than a matter of miles. He found disunity, apathy and uncertainty. For thousands of years, the various approaches to religion in India had been loosely defined, with no rigid central dogma; but sectarianism had begun to form in defence against organized and uncompromising Islam after the Muslim invasion. In the twilight of Muslim rule, confusion and superstition, rites, rituals, a greedy priesthood, and sect versus sect within Hinduism, racked the religion of the country. Then came British rule; lawlessness was suppressed and efficiency imposed, but this too was an alien culture. Christian missionaries regarded the Hindus as heathen, and taught them to doubt their own gods; while religious doubts and cynicism from the West influenced the students at the universities.

Ramkumar was appointed priest of the Kali temple in the

temple garden recently created by the rich widow Rani Rasmani, at Dakshineswar on the banks of the Ganges four miles north of Calcutta. Gadadhar went with him, though without enthusiasm. The priesthood was not regarded with much respect by the sincerely religious. There was no organized church in the Christian sense; the deepest religion centred on meditation and the simple rituals within the home, or in the totally detached life of a monk, owning nothing. Visiting temples was what might be called today 'an optional extra'. The priests, who were paid, were only too often worldly or corrupt, and repeated the daily rituals parrot-fashion.

When Gadadhar was twenty, loss and grief struck again. Ramkumar died. Gadadhar's religious fervour had caught the attention, approval, and later, the veneration of Mathur Babu, the son-in-law of Rani Rasmani, who administered the estate. He begged Gadadhar to become the priest of the Kali temple. Gadadhar accepted, reluctantly. For two years he became priest; and though eventually he gave up the priestly duties, he continued to live in one simple room in the temple garden for the remaining thirty years of his life. It was probably Mathur who gave him the name Ramakrishna by which he was ever afterwards to be known. Gadadhar the village boy and Gadadhar the priest had both gone. Ramakrishna was now entering on his life's purpose.

It was the purpose which had drawn him from boyhood, the purpose which had been a part of Indian religious thinking for thousands of years; the realization (and the use of that word implies a full experience, not an intellectual realization, just as seeing a colour is an experience, not an intellectual acceptance that colour exists) of what has many names in many languages – God, 'That', the Ultimate, the Lord. It is the opening of a new faculty, the discovery of what Man in fact *is*. In Christian terms, 'Now I see in a glass darkly, but then face to face'. This is not regarded in Hinduism as something that may, perhaps, happen after death, but – again in Christian terms – 'In this flesh shall I see God'. There was no implication that everyone was ready for the experience, or that there was only one path to it. The belief in reincarnation taught that we are all at different stages, some would advance slowly, some swiftly, the seed in each soul would open when it was ripe. His later great disciple, Vivekananda, said that if he himself had to chose between truth and God, he would choose truth. His Master went further : truth, which *is*

God, in full experience and beyond doubt; or death.

The three temples in the temple garden (the Siva temple consists in fact of twelve small temples) represent and sum up in themselves the main Hindu attitude to life, to the cosmos, to the individual and his place in the world in which he finds himself; the answer to the ageless question, the question of identity : 'What is existence? What am I?'

The great god of renunciation, Siva, represents Ultimate Brahman; That which *is*; beyond name and form. Of this, we are all manifestations; the One mistakenly regarding Itself as many; Ramakrishna later said that Brahman is the one thing that has never been defiled by the lips of man, for no words can describe It. The experience of universal, contentless consciousness – Satchidananda (Existence, Knowledge, Bliss absolute – has been sought in India for thousands of years. The West has perhaps tended to regard as either illusory, poetic, or at most something to be glimpsed by mystics or attained after death, any experience or view of life which reveals that Man is immeasurably greater than he thinks.

The word 'mistakenly' sounds a little odd in this context; if I am 'That', why do I regard myself as separate, frustrated, over-busy, anxious? Why, if I am ill, do I identify myself with a body about which the only thing I really know without question is that I shall one day leave it?

The answer to these questions lay, for Ramakrishna, in the Kali mother-figure. In the statue within the Kali temple, Siva lies unmoving; he projects 'maya', the cosmic illusion in which we are all caught – Kali, the mother, dances, and her dance is beautiful and terrible. She is the paradox by which the One appears as many; she is time, she is death, she is the finite ego; she is both good and evil, suffering and joy; she is here worshipped as Bhavatarini, the saviour of the universe. She is, above all, cosmic energy; through her we reach Siva, the Ultimate. In her left pair of hands she holds a sword and severed head; her right hands bestow protection and blessing. Good and evil are seen as two sides of the same coin; evil and the terrible are accepted without fear or repulsion, but it is through dedicating himself to the highest moral good that Man reaches Brahman at last, though the play of 'the Mother' at first deludes him.

The third temple is devoted to a personal approach to God which is especially suited to natures which are loving and emotional rather than austere and world-renouncing, and for those who are 'in the world' rather than monastic. This is the approach of Bhakti Yoga, and it is symbolized in the Radhakanta temple, in the love between Radha (the human soul) and Krishna (God); here there is a sense of Dualism, of the soul separate from Godhead but loving and serving God, as in Christian worship the soul approaches God through love of Jesus, or of God seen as Father.

Now began the hidden years of mystical experience; twelve years which can only be briefly touched upon here. Was the Mother a reality or simply a symbol, a beautiful concept? Ramakrishna spent days and nights in meditation in a jungle to the north of the temples; in agony of mind he would rub his face against the ground and weep bitterly. Sleep left him; he ate only enough to remain alive. At last, he could stand no more. Nothing else in life mattered. He saw the sword that was kept in the Kali temple. In his own words :

I determined to put an end to my life. When I jumped up like a madman and seized the sword, suddenly the blessed Mother revealed herself. The buildings with their different parts, the temple and everything else vanished from my sight, leaving no trace whatsoever, and in their stead I saw a limitless, effulgent stream of consciousness. What was happening in the outside world I did not know, but within me there was a steady flow of undiluted bliss, altogether new, and I felt the presence of the Divine Mother.

After that, as far as the temple officials were concerned, he became for a time quite mad. They complained bitterly. Mathur Babu did not agree. He and his wife watched discreetly, and came to the conclusion that here they had found a jewel which must at all costs be preserved. They had already found in Rama-krishna a passion of devotion to God, a beautiful voice in singing the holy songs, strength of character, love, compassion and humour; these were human characteristics and they valued them in him; they respected him; they were fond of him. But now he was going far beyond human characteristics into entirely new realms.

The tendency of the people around him either to declare him insane, or to fall at his feet, was not even noticed by Ramakrishna, who began to see the Mother both in the temple statue and as a real person who spoke to him, and lived. The vision was not constant; it was as though he was moving between different planes, and sometimes went beyond the personal. On one such occasion, he fed a cat with the food that was to be offered to Kali in the temple. This was more than the manager of the garden could stand, and he reported it to Mathur. Ramakrishna explained:

The Divine Mother revealed to me that it was She who had become everything. She showed me that everything was full of consciousness. I found everything inside the room soaked, as it were, in bliss. The bliss of God. I saw a wicked man in front of the Kali temple, but in him also I saw the power of the Divine Mother vibrating. That was why I fed a cat with the food that was to be offered . . . I clearly saw that all this was the Divine Mother – even the cat.

In the West the feeding of the cat might be regarded as whimsical; in India it cut clear across ritual observances regarding the clean and the unclean, especially as regards animals, and animals in temples; Ramakrishna respected and observed all religious customs; his explanation was revolutionary. It was also unanswerable.

In the teachings of his later years, the animal kingdom was often used in illustrations of homely – and often very funny – parables to illustrate the deepest truths of the spiritual life. The most profound philosophy and theology he sometimes interspersed with parables concerning snakes, tigers, dogs, and many more, including two pompous and bigoted frogs in whom Disney might well have rejoiced. One of his disciples, after his Master's death, was told by a woman devotee that a mother cat brought her kittens to Ramakrishna's bed, and he could not bear to have them removed, for they had come to him for protection. Finally he asked her to take them and care for them, and asked always about their welfare, for all things as well as all people must be loved, served, and if helpless, protected, as in them all God was manifest.

He also later used an illustration from the animal world (perhaps it was based on that very cat!) to show that there are two different natures among spiritual aspirants. One, he said, has the nature of the baby monkey, with an inborn instinct to cling to the neck of the mother as she jumps from tree to tree. The other has the nature of the baby kitten whose instinct is to rely solely on the mother and to remain where she places it. 'Sometimes she places it in the ashes, and sometimes on the master's bed', he said; if help is needed, the kitten mews to its mother. This is not a matter of over-activity on the one hand and inertia on the other – indeed, he warned against both – it represents the nature of total faith in one case, and in the other, a nature which feels that for spiritual progress, certain things must be done, or certain ritual performed; it may even lead to the Jnani nature which casts the world from him. But it is an exact illustration from the animal kingdom, of an inborn spiritual tendency in different people which must be recognized and accepted, and which they themselves must work out to the full, as part of the great harmony in which all souls do not play the same note, on the same instrument, in exactly the same way.

Meanwhile, in Kamarpukur, Ramakrishna's own mother was becoming anxious. Confused reports had reached her regarding her son's sanity. He returned to the village for a while, but spent most of the time in meditation. Nothing else interested him at this stage. He was twenty-three years old; with his agreement, his mother arranged a marriage for him, by which was meant a betrothal to a child who would come to him as a wife in later years, as was customary.

He was married to a little girl of five, Saradamani, who lived in the neighbouring village of Jayrambati, and then he returned to the temple garden at Dakshineswar, leaving Sarada with her mother. In later years she came to him as his first disciple, spiritual consort, and wife, but the marriage remained for ever sexually unconsummated, since these two were by nature monk and nun, each with the great self-discipline of the yogi who uses the sexual force in meditation, and would become bound to the body rather than detached from it by sexual emotion. Ramakrishna knew that continence is a necessity for the highest states of God-realization, but he was not advocating celibacy for the whole of mankind, or even for all his followers, any more than he expected them all to attempt – still worse, to imitate – the full experiences of his own spiritual path.

On his return to Dakshineswar, the 'divine madness' came upon him again. To root out of himself any idea of caste superiority, he cleaned the house of an outcaste with his own hair, which for a time had grown long and neglected. He sat for days in meditation; birds perched on his head and he did not know that they were there; snakes crawled over him and neither was aware of the other.

An elderly Brahmin woman, an adept in the Tantrik and Vaishnava methods of worship, came to Dakshineswar. It was she who assured him that he was not mad, and who assembled the pundits and theologians who finally declared him to be an Incarnation – which did not impress him with any sense of his own importance. Under her tuition, he practised all the disciplines of the sixty-four Tantras, in which sense-objects are deified, but without the permitted wine and sex-relations which had caused degradation in some cases. He was proving at every step, in one life, that all paths could lead to the same great fulfilment.

The third stage of his spiritual journey led him to the path he so often later advised for those still living 'in the world' and involved in busy life and human relationships; the assuming of a close personal, human relationship with God, as a Christian does in his love for God as father, for Mary as mother, or Jesus as friend or master. These Bhavas, or attitudes to God, are particularly designed to break down, by degrees, the awe which brings a sense of distance and separation; God is worshipped as master, as friend, as a tiny child (as we see in the Christian Christmas) and as a lover or spouse (again, a common link can be seen with the Christian nun's 'bride of Christ') and in each case he found the great experience along paths which are usually assumed to apply to differing natures.

All that he had experienced so far, however, still left some separation, however slight, between the soul and God. Now he was ready for the heights of Advaita Vedanta, in which the aspirant goes beyond the experience of a personal God, to pure Being without form or attributes, to become That which is, beyond words and beyond description. A monk called Totapuri came to him; after forty years of spiritual practices, he had achieved Nirvikalpa samadhi, the state of contentless consciousness. He instructed Ramakrishna, who had no difficulty in withdrawing his mind from all objects except one : 'The form of the blissful Mother, radiant and the essence of divine consciousness'. In despair he tried again and again, but he could not pass beyond her, and he told Totapuri that it was impossible. Totapuri insisted that he could and must. Pressing a tiny piece of glass between Ramakrishna's eyebrows, he told him to concentrate his mind on that point. This time, as soon as the form of the Mother appeared before him, 'I used my power of discrimination as a sword and with it severed her form in two'. He was at once lost in the super-conscious state.

Totapuri left him alone for three days and three nights, and then found him still in the same state, the face serene and radiant, but with no sign of heart-beat or respiration in the body. Totapuri saw that his disciple had achieved what had taken forty years in his own case. He brought him back to normal consciousness gradually, by the repetition of a mantram, but when Totapuri left Dakshineswar, Ramakrishna again entered the state of Nirvikalpa samadhi, and stayed in that state for six months, kept alive by the kindly help and occasional 'force feeding' of a monk who was staying there. When he finally returned to normal life, he believed that he had received the command to remain on the threshold of relative consciousness, for the sake of humanity, which meant that for the rest of his life he moved, as it were, between the different planes of consciousness, able to play any note in the great harmony, speaking to each person who came to him in that person's spiritual language, and even in his most human and light-hearted moods, always a child of his divine Mother God, as well as one who could dwell on the heights. In all mankind he saw God made manifest, and no longer separate from himself; service to Man was not philanthropy, but the joy of service to God, manifest in all that existed.

In his desire to experience all religions he also practised the religious observances of Christianity and of Islam, putting aside for a while all Hindu observances and ideas. In each case he reached the same goal, and became convinced of the truth of both. He was devoted to Buddha, and to the beliefs of the Sikhs and the Jains. He was the first great mystic and teacher to experience the truth of all religions and to teach that all Truth is one; that all religions are one religion, manifesting itself in various forms to suit different natures or different countries.

None of his teachings, however, pointed to a sentimental eclecticism in which the more attractive (and usually the easier) portions of all the world religions are taken and muddled together. He preached a harmony of all religions, philosophies, and approaches, in all nations, in an orchestra in which each, so to speak, plays his own instrument as perfectly as he can, but without enmity – or without even the slight condescension which is sometimes called tolerance – towards the other instruments and chords in the whole harmony. And certainly there must be no suggestion that, in the end, all must come to play exactly the same tune on exactly the same instrument. The agnostic or atheist who was sincerely seeking, in complete honesty, he welcomed; when the bud was ready, it would open, there must be no forcing; people were at very different stages. His love and his acceptance were boundless, but on certain fundamentals he stood adamant. Absolute truth and honesty were vital; all progress must rest on a basis of moral purity, and if people would not accept this, then let them not claim a purity which was not theirs. To a man who explained the reason for his great number of children by claiming that they were not the result of his self-indulgent sexuality, but conceived as a religious duty, to raise up progeny in respect for his ancestors, he remarked drily, 'Never commit perjury in the shrine of sentiment'. Lust, and greed for money, he regarded as the great enemies of all spiritual progress; both appeared to offer an illusory freedom and pleasure, both brought a terrible bondage. Bigotry was the destroyer of all harmonies.

Although he was a man of great gentleness, he insisted on strength and 'grit'; he said there must be nothing 'mushy'; prayer and longing would bring strength and faith. He had no time for sloppiness; in everyday living he liked simplicity, neatness and order, and disliked vagueness; he said, 'A man should have dignity and alertness'.

His compassion for those in spiritual need extended also to those in physical distress. On a pilgrimage with the wealthy Mathur Babu, he found people starving in a famine area, and insisted that they should be fed and clothed. When Mathur objected, Ramakrishna sat down with the people and said that he would stay there and share their miseries. Mathur yielded, as he did on another occasion when Ramakrishna insisted that Mathur's tenants, who were suffering hopeless poverty as a result of failed harvests, should have their rents remitted, and should be fed. This was not philanthropy, which he mistrusted because it often led to egotism; this was the serving of God made manifest in one's fellow-men, for whatever one had been given – spirituality, or talent, education or money – was not something one owned, but something to be held in trust and freely shared or given.

Now that twelve years of spiritual search and discovery were over, the great men of his day, as well as humble seekers, began to come to him. In particular the famous leader of the Brahmo Samaj – Keshab Sen – was attracted to and influenced by the personality and teachings of Ramakrishna, whom he regarded as a saint. There was deep respect and friendship between them, and much discussion. For the first time, Ramakrishna, a Hindu of Hindus, without knowledge of the ideas and influence of the West, began to see that new religious movements, like the Brahmo Samaj, were springing up and influencing the educated middle classes, especially through the universities, though they did not reach the mass of the people. They were sincerely struggling to reconcile many ideas which were almost irreconcilable – accepting or rejecting the influence of Christianity, rebelling against the Hindu worship of the many gods, establishing belief in a personal God of varying definition, hoping to raise the status of women and reform the caste system. Intellectual arguments raged. Devendranath Tagore, the father of Rabindranath, the poet, fought to stop the infiltration of Christian ideas into the Samaj. He was the enemy of image worship; Keshab Sen himself fluctuated between Christ and the Divine Mother of Hinduism. Ideas were in a ferment.

Ramakrishna was impressed by their sincerity, and saw that they were trying to make the eternal compromise between religion and worldly living. He did not force his ideas upon them, but told them to take from him as little or as much as they needed. His influence on them led them to a greater acceptance of the various forms of religion, including the symbols of Hinduism, and deepened their thinking about the harmony of religions. Some of his eventual disciples from the universities were young students who had originally been attracted to the Brahmo Samaj and still respected it, but were seeking a deep experience and certainty rather than the ferment of even the noblest ideas.

Now Ramakrishna began to long for his own devotees and disciples, for those who would remain with him and become his spiritual companions and with whom he could share all the fruits of his years of spiritual experience, at a deeper level than was possible with enquirers who came and went. In intense longing, he cried, 'Come, my children! Where are you? I cannot bear to live without you'. And one by one, during the last six years of his life, they came, both those who later became monks and those who were married.

His first disciple had been his wife, Sarada, who came to him as a young woman of eighteen. She had willingly accepted his dedication to his life of celibacy. She was gentle, unselfish and withdrawn, in her veiled life of purdah. Ramakrishna did not advocate a life of seclusion for all women, but this was her nature, and, when at Dakshineswar, she stayed in the seclusion of a small stone building called a 'nahabat', originally used for religious music, where she lived, slept and cooked. At one time she also cared for his old mother who came to live near her son in the upper room of the nahabat, and died there. Ramakrishna instructed his young wife and spiritual companion in everything from housekeeping to the knowledge of Brahman, and the deepest realities of spiritual life. On one occasion he worshipped her as the Divine Mother made manifest, seeing especially in her, as he saw in all women, the motherhood of God. She spent much of her time with her own mother and family in her home village, and her uncomplaining life of hard work in the village, combined with the spiritual heights she attained, and the motherly love she gave to all who came to her, as well as her quiet dignity and gentle sense of fun, made her much loved and sometimes worshipped by devotees. The name by which she is still known – 'The Holy Mother' – was appropriate to her life and character. She lived for more than thirty years after the death of her husband, and, still withdrawn in purdah, became known in Calcutta as a great spiritual figure, tirelessly available to all who came to her in weariness and distress. She became one of the great lamps who kept alight the life and teachings of Ramakrishna, and she regarded the young monks as her spiritual sons, and encouraged them in establishing the work of spiritual teaching and the relief of suffering which still goes on today. Like her husband, she avoided fuss, publicity, or the founding of a sect; her love went to all, silently and always in the background.

The last six years of Ramakrishna's life, in which he gave to those who came to him the great teachings which summed up his life's experience, giving each enquirer as much or as little as was needed, and from many points of view to suit many different natures, were later recorded by a disciple, Mahendranath Gupta, known as 'M', headmaster of the Vidyasagar High School in Calcutta. He recorded not only the teaching and conversation he heard on his frequent visits to the room in the temple garden in Dakshineswar, but the expression on his Master's face, his comments, his jokes, even the movement of the moonlight on the water of the Ganges. Never has a great teacher, prophet, saint, mystic, Incarnation (and Ramakrishna has been regarded as many things, by many people, so his title should be left open, as he himself said that, like a loving mother, he gave different food to different children, and made no vast public claims for himself), never has a great religious figure been so faithfully recorded. 'M' came to him a little shyly at first, awed by the great serenity, austerity and spiritual ecstasy of this man who was unlike anyone he had ever met. Then he found Ramakrishna full of fun and laughter, and as he sat nervously in the corner of the room, Ramakrishna remarked, 'You see, he is a little advanced in years, and therefore somewhat serious. He sits quiet while the youngsters make merry.' 'M' was twenty-eight at the time.

When at last Ramakrishna lay dying, he was removed to a house nearer Calcutta where he could be nursed and cared for by his disciples with the help of Sarada Devi. So many people came to him now for advice and teaching that his throat cancer worsened as he continued to teach them, for even when he could only speak by signs, he answered their questions. Powers in him which in the West would be called miraculous or psychic, he had always regarded as natural manifestations on certain planes and at certain stages of spirituality, but had warned against them as being stumbling stones in the direct path to God-vision; he had never been a 'miracle-monger'. In his last days, his spiritual states and his love for all overflowed all bounds; a typical comment afterwards, from one who came to see him was that he had felt as frank and free with him 'as if we had been classmates . . . but as soon as I left his presence, then it flashed on me – "think where I have been!" '

This visitor, Aswini Kumar Dutta, who was deeply respected at that time as one of the saintly patriots of Bengal, wrote in a letter to 'M', that on one occasion, when talking to Ramakrishna, who was giving him spiritual advice, Dutta said to him, 'You are full of fun! There is great fun in your company!' Ramakrishna laughed, and said, 'Well said! Right you are!' Then he told Dutta of his own religious austerities, and described to him the self-control and renunciation which were the other side of the joy and laughter which made him so happy in the company of children, and which brought to him moods where he encouraged his young disciples in picnics and tree-climbing; moods in which the great scholars who came to him for his teachings were soon laughing at his jokes as well.

He often likened his states of religious ecstasy to an intoxication which was indescribable but full of unwavering spiritual bliss.

Sri Ramakrishna

He explained to Dutta that householders, with their many duties in the world, cannot forsake everything and become so inebriated with the thought of God that all normal consciousness drops from them; nevertheless – 'Since you are going to lead a householder's life, create a roseate intoxication in your mind with the thought of God. You will be doing your duties, but let that intoxication remain with you.'

The teaching that daily meditation combined with a life in which the thought of God – Personal or Impersonal, He or That – glows always at the back of the mind like a serene and joyful spiritual intoxication, was followed by the other great precept which healed the anxiety which frets at us all. 'As long as you live in the world, give God the power of attorney. Make over all your responsibilities to Him; let Him do as He likes.' This, taken out of context, could imply an evasion of work and responsibility, and so was followed by the illustration he so often gave, of the maidservant working in her master's house. Practical as always, and with homely illustrations, he countered the difficulty of working in a master's house without becoming too much identified with it – as we all do – by pointing out that before handling anything sticky, the hands must be smeared with something which will protect them. 'Protect yourself with the oil of devotion, then the world will not cling to you and you will not be affected by it.' Dutta adds, 'I cannot express in words how much I enjoyed his company that day.' Dutta was not a close disciple or devotee, he writes that he saw Ramakrishna not more than four or five times, '. . . But in that short time we became so intimate that I felt as if we had been class-mates. What I saw and received in those few days has sweetened my whole life.'

Girish Ghosh, the great Bengali dramatist and father of the modern Bengali stage, was in his early life a sceptic, a drinker, a man euphemistically labelled 'a great sinner'. He became one of Ramakrishna's most devoted disciples. Ramakrishna never compromised on his own asceticism, and his rejection of drinking, sexual promiscuity, and everything else which chains Man to his own weakness and his own ego. But he saw within Girish the heroic figure of near-saintliness which, after a lifetime's struggle, he finally became. Without condoning the faults of this disciple, he saw the potential which lay beneath the faults. What in others he might have rebuked, in Girish he forgave, and treated with a love that was almost maternal.

B

It was told that one night Girish and two friends, very drunk, left a 'house of ill-fame' and went to Ramakrishna at Dakshineswar, where, in spiritual ecstasy, he danced with them. The impression this made on Girish – to find the man whom Girish worshipped as an Incarnation of God, dancing with the three drunkards by the temple near the sacred Ganges – is reminiscent of the story of Christ at the wedding feast, or Christ accepting the anointing of his feet by the sinner, Mary Magdalene. It was a question of recognition; the great lamp in the disciple was almost ready to show its light. Indeed, when Girish was unable to find regular time for meditation because of his irregular hours in the theatre, Ramakrishna said, 'Give me your power of attorney'. This sounded easy, but in fact from then on, Girish was constantly thinking of Ramakrishna, and examining his own thoughts and actions to make sure that they were Guru-and-God centred. After Ramakrishna's death, Girish had to face the death of his son, of his wife, and bankruptcy. He gave up drink and opium, and after many struggles became a figure of great spiritual stature, much loved and respected.

As Ramakrishna was dying, his samadhi of supreme spiritual communion, his teaching, and his laughter, continued; so did his love and his practicality, both in his stricter instruction to those who would become monks, and in his understanding of those still scorched by the world and its duties and relationships. The last incident 'M' records of him, tells of an occasion three months before his death, when 'M' brought his wife, who was torn with grief by the death of one of her sons, to see him. The dying man did not preach her a sermon about death. He questioned her tenderly about her household, and asked her to come again and to spend a few days with Sarada Devi, the 'Holy Mother'. He did not forget to ask about her baby daughter, though with his throat cancer he could hardly speak.

When Ramakrishna died in 1886, he left no money and no property. But he left something more important – people. He left a group of disciples, mostly young men without a monastery, without money, and apparently without much future. Some of them were already breaking away from university, home, or career, because with Ramakrishna they had found their life's purpose. He left married devotees, men and women, who could not forget what Ramakrishna had brought to them, and who could not bear to let his truths and experience end there. He left Sarada Devi, who lived on for thirty years after his death; he left 'M' with his notes, his memories, and his book, *The Gospel of Sri Ramakrishna*, still to be written. He left many who knew him and were willing to record all that they knew and remembered while there was still time.

He also left a young man of eighteen called Narendranath Datta, usually known as Naren, who was later to be known throughout India, America, England, and in many countries of the world, as Swami Vivekananda.

2

VIVEKANANDA

After the first shock of grief following the death of Ramakrishna, the young disciples were left uncertain and distraught, until a lay disciple offered to rent a house at Barangore which could be a temporary monastery for the young monks, and which the married devotees could visit for peace and meditation. This might have been expected. What would have been more surprising to anyone who had not witnessed those last, vital formative years with Ramakrishna, was the way Naren was immediately accepted as elder brother, father-figure, organizer and tower of strength, like an heir to a kingdom who has already been trained, appointed, loved and prepared by the dying head of the kingdom. And if that kingdom had to begin, at first, in a dreary old tumble-down house populated with snakes and lizards and avoided by other tenants because it was believed to be haunted, at least it was cheap. If nobody could afford clothes, one respectable garment had to be held in common so that whoever went out could go decently clad; if on some days there was nothing to eat, and on others a little rice without salt, and boiled leaves of the Bimba creeper; so much the better for those whose watchword was 'renunciation' and who were on fire to carry forward what had been begun.

They installed a few simple relics of their Master; worship, prayer, singing, and intense austerities went on constantly; sometimes the young monks sat unmoving in meditation day and night. Naren insisted on the study of modern philosophies, as well as the teachings of Christ and Buddha: they studied Hegel, Kant and Mill; they analysed theories of atheism. Those of them who lived to be old men always recalled the 'Barangore days' as the first great beginnings which burned with a passion of spiritual fire which they never afterwards forgot.

Naren himself, before he came to Ramakrishna, became known at the University as a cigar-smoking young cynic who shocked the conventional. A fellow-student wrote of him, during that earlier period :

He took an almost morbid delight in shocking conventionality in its tabernacles, respectability in its booths . . . he cried out for a hand to save, to uplift, to protect – a Guru or Master who by embodying perfection in the flesh would still the commotion in his soul. He had enough, he bitterly complained, of moral disquisitions, principles, intuitions for pabulum which seemed to him tasteless and insipid.

His childhood background could not have been more different from Kamarpukur and the youth of Ramakrishna, but the similarities are as striking as the differences. His father was an attorney in the High Court of Calcutta, an agnostic who studied the Christian Bible; a man of compassion who gave almost too generously to his relatives; so much so that on his death the family was left nearly destitute, while the same relatives tried to claim even the family house; Naren's cynicism about the ways of the world was not without foundation. His mother was a deeply religious woman with a prodigious memory which Naren inherited. She was particularly kind to the poor and helpless. Naren's memory we should probably now label 'total recall'; at seven he could repeat from memory the whole of a Sanskrit Grammar, and passages of enormous length from the Hindu epics; as a man, after reading *Pickwick Papers* twice, he could repeat whole chapters from it. (Like Ramakrishna, his sense of humour was one of his outstanding characteristics; 'Pickwick', 'Punch' and 'Alice' were delights to him later; he always regretted not having written a book like 'Alice' for children.) As a child, Naren was restless, brilliant and mischievous; like his Master, he was devoted to wandering monks, and had to be locked away when they came asking for alms, or he would have given them all he had. Deep meditation was natural to him, and when, every night, he saw a spot of light which shone between his eyebrows and then expanded into a flood of light which covered his whole body until he fell asleep, he did not connect this in any way with inner powers of meditation; he simply assumed that everybody fell asleep like that.

As a boy of eight he attended Vidyasagar's Metropolitan Institution. He was friendly with every family in the neighbourhood, both high and low caste; his energy led him to jumping, running, boxing, fencing, organizing plays and athletics, rowing, wrestling, cooking, even the making of toy gas-works. At sixteen he entered college and eventually gained his BA degree and began to study music and law. It was at college that he first heard of Ramakrishna. Professor William Hastie, a famous scholar of his day, was explaining Wordsworth's 'Excursion', in which Wordsworth refers to the depth of spiritual experience which can arise from a glimpse of nature's beauty, but only if combined with a very rare type of concentration and purity of mind. Hastie told Naren that he himself had only met one human being who had experienced that state of mind fully. 'He is Ramakrishna Paramahamsa of Dakshineswar. You can understand if you go there and see for yourself.'

Naren hesitated. He had for some time been strongly attracted to the Brahmo Samaj. Most of young Bengal, especially from the colleges, was flocking there. The Samaj, under the leadership of Keshab Sen, who had organized it originally with Devendranath Tagore, father of the poet Rabindranath Tagore, was struggling against the superstitions which had gripped Hinduism, and was much influenced by the thinking of the British rulers. It was struggling to follow many different paths at once, many of them much needed, but this was leading to confusion and splinter-groups. It protested against polytheism, image worship, divine Incarnations, or the need for a Guru, and worshipped a personal God (as distinct from the Absolute of Vendanta) and thus left no freedom of choice as to how God or reality was to be experienced. There were differences of opinion about Jesus; and it advocated social reform in the caste system, child-marriage, and the emancipation of women. Naren was drawn to many of its ideas, but he wanted truth and practicality. Had it the power to carry out social reforms? Obviously, no. And the passion for spiritual experience which drew him to the Samaj, required an answer to the sixty-four-thousand dollar question – the *only* question – 'Are these still theories, attempts to describe the indescribable? Have they brought to anyone the *experience* of God?' Naren was not one to beat about the bush. He went to Devendranath Tagore, then living in retirement on a boat on the Ganges, and put his question, 'Sir – have you seen God?'

Devendranath was an honest man. He looked long at Naren and said, 'My son, you have the Yogi's eyes. You must meditate.'

Deeply disappointed, Naren put his question to the leaders of other sects. The answer, in all honesty, was always 'No'. So, remembering what he had been told of a man called Ramakrishna, he went to Dakshineswar.

The chief shock of surprise in his first meeting with Ramakrishna lay in the discovery that he was expected. Ramakrishna had long been expecting a great soul to come to him, who would carry his work forward. He was then in his forties, and had already seen Naren in a vision; and when the young cynic, who did not believe in visions, walked into the room, he recognized him at once, and, to Naren's amazement, took him away from the others in the room, and asked him eagerly why he had kept him waiting so long. He showed so much love, welcome and delighted recognition that Naren came to the conclusion that this man, who seemed to him the most spiritually advanced human being he had ever met, was unfortunately quite mad, and probably a monomaniac. The monomaniac asked him if he saw a light between his brows before he fell asleep, and was delighted (but not surprised) to hear that he did. At last, Naren put to him his great question – 'Sir, have you seen God?' And he received the immediate answer : 'Yes. I see Him just as I see you here, but in a much intenser sense.'

One thing impressed Naren deeply. This man, mad or not, was not speaking from theory, but from experience. It was also clear that he did not preach renunciation while keeping one finger on worldly comfort or fame; he lived out whatever he said, one hundred per cent.

This drew him back again, a month later. This time, Ramakrishna, by a touch, gave Naren an experience of the Ultimate; Naren, in terror, felt plunged into an experience for which he was not ready; he felt that he was facing death, and shouted a protest. Ramakrishna gently returned him to his usual state of consciousness and said, 'All right. Let it rest now. Everything will come in time.'

On Naren's third visit to Dakshineswar, Ramakrishna himself entered into a trance state. This time Naren lost consciousness altogether, and when he regained it he could remember nothing of what had happened. Ramakrishna made no comment, but much later he said that while Naren was unconscious he had put questions to him which he had answered from the depth of his true Self, and his answers had confirmed that this was indeed a great sage in the making, born a master of meditation, who would serve the world, and that the day he knew his real nature, he would give up his body in death, by an act of will, through yoga.

No other disciple was treated in this way; each was helped gently and gradually along his own path; from now on Naren, with the others, listened and learned and experienced. For the remaining five years of Ramakrishna's life, this young sceptic who at first regarded the idea that Man is a manifestation of God, as yet ignorant of his true identity, as little short of blasphemy, who doubted the Hindu gods, detested Kali and disliked the idea of a guru, came to Ramakrishna as his disciple with a growing love, veneration, and a conviction that here at last was truth, plus a determination to fight for his own intellect and common sense every inch of the way. This tendency Ramakrishna encouraged, for he, too, had fought long battles, not with his intellect but with his soul and body in the long lonely years when he had struggled for spiritual experience. Sincerity was Ramakrishna's bedrock, his watchword; without total sincerity and what he called 'guilelessness', all was useless. So Naren loved, respected, fretted, argued, doubted and questioned; at first he was held mainly by love, for he said that never in his life, even from his parents, had he received such love, or seen such love given to all who came, and to all humanity. Never had he seen such selflessness or childlike lack of pride combined with such serene strength; he came simply because this man was as he was; he was not yet fully convinced.

He made frequent visits and listened with others to the great teachings of philosophy and mysticism and the practicalities of everyday life. He laughed and played with other youngsters too, for often there were jokes and laughter, singing of holy songs, and sometimes picnics and tree-climbing, or a visit to the Star Theatre where a great religious story was being presented, for one of Ramakrishna's famous disciples was Girish Ghosh, the greatest Bengali dramatist of his time, the father of modern Bengali drama.

To live in the constant companionship of one who had 'realized' – that is, experienced – God, and whose states of trance, many times each day, brought not some weird fantasy-living, but an increasing strength of character and an increasing holiness of personality, was certainly what Naren had been seeking, but it was not to be easy. With Naren, and only with him, Ramakrishna encouraged the study of Advaita Vedanta, which goes to the heights of the Absolute, and includes all other paths. His daily life, too, was to be tough and hard and lived under constant strain, and the schooling for that, also, began early.

In 1884 Naren's father died suddenly of a heart attack. The family was plunged into poverty; creditors arrived; relatives tried to take even their house from the destitute family. Naren now had seven or eight people dependent on him, and no income. He had passed his BA but was only beginning to study law; he went from office to office in search of work, and often pretended that he had eaten in some friend's house so that the family should have what little food there was. He took a temporary teaching post in Vidyasagar's school; he was learning the bitter fact that the innocent can, in fact, starve. At that time, when one of his friends sang a song about the grace of God, Naren replied that such songs were only suitable for those who were born with a silver spoon in their mouths, and had no starving relatives at home. In his own later words, 'I was exceedingly cross with God!'

One evening, in the season of the rains, worn out after a day's search for work, soaked by rain and unfed, he fell exhausted on a doorstep on his way home. Suddenly, a deep new experience came to him.

All my former doubts regarding the co-existence of divine justice and mercy in the creation of a blissful providence, were automatically solved. By a deep introspection I found the meaning of it all and was satisfied. As I proceeded homewards I found that there was no trace of fatigue in the body and the mind was refreshed with wonderful strength and peace.

Later, he – who had never been able to bring himself to pray to the gods – asked his Master to pray to 'the Divine Mother' for him, but Ramakrishna sent him to the Kali temple to pray, for himself, not through an intermediary. And there he experienced 'the Divine Mother, living and conscious' and this experience so transformed him that he asked Ramakrishna to teach him a song in her praise, which he sang in joy all night, and in the morning slept on the porch outside his Master's room.

This did not bring an easy floating on clouds in continual bliss; it was as though a new faculty had opened, a glimpse of reality given, a milestone passed. For a while he had experienced Truth, and had discovered that Godhead may be personal as well as impersonal; 'God is really impersonal, but seen through the mists of the senses, becomes personal', said Ramakrishna.

As the end approached, watching his dying Master he saw, as he had seen throughout the five years with him, a loving, suffering human being who still constantly moved into states of samadhi; a blending of the human and the divine. In particular, he watched his ever-increasing love for humanity, a love which had passed the bounds of the human tenderness and compassion which they all saw so often in Ramakrishna, and was clearly a primal force which recognized exactly the same Godhead in himself as in others, and as clearly in others as in himself. When unable to eat because of his throat cancer, he felt that the Mother was rebuking him for wanting food : 'You are eating through all these mouths'. Earlier, Ramakrishna had said – recognizing the Self both in himself and in a disciple –

Now and then a man catches a glimpse of his real Self and becomes speechless with wonder. At such times he swims in an ocean of joy. It is like suddenly meeting a dear relative. The other day . . . I felt like that at the sight of Baburam, also. When Siva realizes his own Self, he dances in joy.

Naren did not hope to create a world of Ramakrishnas, but he said :

How beautifully has he reconciled the ideal of Bhakti [devotion to God] with the knowledge of Vedanta [the world-renouncing 'oneness with the Absolute']. What a grand natural, and sweet synthesis . . . I have understood that the ideal of Vedanta lived by the recluse outside the pale of society can be practised from hearth and home and applied to all our daily schemes of life. Whatever may be the vocation of a man, let him understand and realize that it is God alone who has manifested Himself as the world and created beings. He is both immanent and transcendent. It is He who has become all diverse creatures, objects of our love, respect or compassion, and yet He is beyond all these.

He began to see that the sharing of truth as he had found it here was to be his life's work.

He still longed for the great experience of Nirvikalpa samadhi, to become one with the Absolute and to remain in that state for several days. He begged Ramakrishna to give it to him. Ramakrishna rebuked him and said, 'There is a state higher than that, even. Do you not sing, "Thou are all there is"?' Naren was to help others: his own individual liberation he must regard as relatively insignificant. But one evening, quite unexpectedly, when Naren was meditating, he felt a light at the back of his head and merged wholly in that light. He experienced Nirvikalpa samadhi and remained for some hours in that state for which there is no description. On return to normal consciousness, peace and ecstasy lingered for a while. Ramakrishna told him that now 'Mother' had shown him everything,

but as a treasure is locked up in a box, so will this experience be locked up and the key will remain with me. You have work to do. When you have finished Mother's work, the treasure box will be unlocked again, and you will know everything then, just as you do now.

Ramakrishna told the other disciples that the veil of the Absolute in Naren was so thin that it might give way at any time, but he had prayed that Naren should be a little 'entangled' in the illusion of maya. When Ramakrishna could no longer speak, he wrote, 'Naren will teach others'. Naren hesitated; he did not desire a life of teaching or lecturing, still less of organizing; he doubted his capabilities also. But his master insisted, 'Your very bones will make you do it.' In the few days that remained, Ramakrishna gave some monastic Gerua clothes and rudraksha rosary beads to some of the young men who were longing to become the monks of the future Order. He gave them a simple ceremony of dedication and placed them in Naren's care.

And so after the death which left them all for a time feeling desolate and orphaned, it was Naren who, after settling a lawsuit which left his family safely established in their own home and, though poor, no longer facing destitution, gathered in the young men to the Barangore monastery, and for three years kept alight there the flame which Ramakrishna had lit. Then, increasingly, the young monks began to feel the need to live for a while the life of a wandering monk, experiencing the hardships of living alone, depending solely on That within them, meditating in solitude, and proving to themselves their own strength of will.

For several years Naren tramped, in all weathers and under all conditions, throughout India, from the Himalayas in the north down to the extreme south. His hardships were appalling, and his health never really recovered; and what he saw nearly broke his heart. The suffering and starvation of the poor; the lives

of the outcastes; four thousand years of a great religion either
degenerated into superstition, or else despised by intellectuals who
were worshipping materialism and who felt no responsibility
whatever for the sufferings of their fellow-citizens. There was an
apathetic acceptance of foreign rule, but no real friendship between British and Indian, who lived side by side almost in
separate glass cases. To the British, the Indians were 'natives' and
'heathen'. To the Indians, the British were 'unclean', and food
touched by them must not be eaten ('cooking pot religion', Naren
called it). His love for his country became his passion. His longing
to relieve the suffering he saw, and to 'call the sleeping god to
awake', as he said, in the nation, as well as in each individual,
tore at him until he was, as a disciple said of him, 'like a lion
caught in a net'.

Sometimes he starved rather than accept a handful of rice from
peasants who, he said, should give it to their children; constantly
he was called back from his wanderings or meditation by the
anxiety caused by illness or need of his brother-monks; his love
for the simple villagers he met made him so many friends that
he had almost to tear himself away, over and over again; his future
course was not at all clear to him. He was welcomed with amazed
delight by high officials, judges, rulers, members of local govern-
ment, scholars, monks and maharajas; especially the maharaja
of Mysore, and the maharaja of Khetri, who became his disciple.
All of them were startled by his knowledge, his learning, his
powers of reason and analysis, which were not at all what they
were accustomed to in wandering monks. He did not speak in
the name of Ramakrishna, nor did he attempt to change or
convert; as his master had said, he 'spoke to each man in his
own language', he took people exactly as he found them and
called out the greatest Self in each, along the lines natural to the
person concerned, but without compromise on essentials. He set
ideas moving, he did not encourage dogma; to the question of
the maharaja of Khetri, 'What is life?' he replied, 'Life is the
unfoldment and development of a being under circumstances
that tend to press it down.' 'And what is education?' 'It is the
nervous association of certain ideas; ideas must be made instincts
before they can become the real possession of consciousness.'

Already he was becoming known. It was suggested that he
should go to America to attend a Parliament of Religions which
was to be held in Chicago, as a representative of Hinduism. At

Hyderabad a huge crowd waited to greet him. He gave a lecture at the college to over a thousand people, including many Europeans. From all sides came offers of money for his fare to America, but still he hesitated. One collection that was made for him, he distributed to the poor. The tragic suicide of his young sister increased his anguish about the fate of women and the poor in India; he longed to bring the spiritual riches of India to the West, and to bring the efficiency, the workers, and financial help from the West to India; each could give the other what it most lacked. But whether the work was for him, he still doubted. He prayed for a sign, and in a dream saw Ramakrishna going ahead of him across the sea, beckoning him to follow. Sarada Devi gave him her blessing. It was the maharaja of Khetri who asked him to take the name 'Vivekananda'. The ending 'ananda' in the name of a monk means 'having the bliss of' and is preceded by a quality or god; 'viveka' means discrimination, in the spiritual sense of discrimination between the real and the unreal, that is, between the eternal and the ephemeral. So, in 1893, Swami Vivekananda sailed to America.

His arrival was hardly what his disciples in India had expected. They thought he had only to appear and all would be well. But the Parliament of Religions did not occur until September and this was July; also it was necessary for delegates to be representatives of an official organization. Hotel prices took all his money; America, the land of schedules and modern travel, utterly confused him. A disciple later wrote :

When he first went to America, it was extremely difficult for him to control the momentum that carried him into meditation. . . . With this habit deeply ingrained, he landed in America, that land of railroads and tramways and complicated engagement lists; and at first it was no uncommon thing for him to be carried two or three times round a tram circuit, only disturbed periodically by the conductor asking for the fare. He was very much ashamed of such occurrences, however, and worked hard to overcome them.

As always, people were drawn to him. Friendships began which lasted for the nine years which he was still to live, as he steadily worked himself to death. The same characteristics in him were remarked upon by everybody who met him, all over the world; a childlike gentleness and immediate friendliness to all who came to him, combined with a toughness and strength which acted like a tonic both on individuals and on his beloved India, for he always stressed 'strength' and 'the god within'; a deep spirituality and a very brilliant intellect which he combined, however, with a refusal to take himself too seriously. When his dignity of manner was described as 'princely', he replied, 'That's not me – that's my walk'. He remarked that the flies and mosquitoes gave him a wide berth, 'because they were very orthodox sabbatarian flies and would not touch a heathen'. At Boston he was asked to address a large audience; distinguished people began to call on him for discussion, amongst them Professor J. H. Wright, professor of Greek at Harvard, who was deeply impressed by Vivekananda and insisted that it was fantastic to ask him for credentials to speak at the Parliament of Religions.

He gave him letters of introduction, which introduced him to the necessary selection committee; he also gave him his fare to Chicago. In Chicago itself, after a series of mishaps which resulted in Vivekananda's sleeping the night in an empty box in the railroad freight yard (which he did not find at all unusual for a wandering monk) more friendships were made, and at last he sat on the platform of the Parliament of Religions with the other delegates, facing audiences which varied daily from seven to ten thousand. When, after many other speakers, he rose to speak, and said simply, 'Sisters and Brothers of America', the entire audience went wild before he could utter another word. He stood, utterly bewildered, as people rose, cheering, to their feet; it was two minutes before he could go on. He spoke, at last, of the universality of religion, quoting, 'Whosoever comes to Me, through whatsoever form, I reach him; all men are struggling through paths which in the end lead to Me.' Later he read his celebrated paper on 'Hinduism' in which he insisted that the aim of life was the overcoming of the small egotistical self, in order to attain infinite, universal individuality. He spoke of 'Oneness', and said the discovery of the Oneness of the Great Self within, the very becoming and being of Divinity, inevitably led to the seeing of the divinity manifest everywhere.

The *Boston Evening Transcript* wrote of him :

On a warm day, when a prosy speaker talked too long and people began going home by hundreds, the chairman would announce that Swami Vivekananda would give a short address just before the benediction. The four thousand fanning people in the Hall of Columbus would sit smiling and expectant, to listen to Vivekananda for fifteen minutes, after an hour or two of other men's speeches.

But this triumph did not elate him. When he was alone, he wept like a child because he saw that his life as an unknown wandering monk was at an end. His hatred of 'name and fame-making' never left him. Once he stopped in the middle of a lecture and walked away. Asked if he felt ill, he said that he had sensed that he held his audience in his hand; they would accept all he said; they were his. 'Which would be bad for them, and very bad for me', he said.

He now embarked on an enormous programme of lecture tours, from the Atlantic coast to the Mississippi river. News came to India that he was introducing Hinduism to the West, and the enthusiasm and pride of his own country reached his fellow-monks. In America, he was not only concerned with lecturing; he felt that much of the interest was inevitably too superficial; he wanted a few serious disciples, not a nine-day-wonder fame. He took a room in a lodging house in New York, and gave classes to small groups of sincere seekers; they sat on the floor, on a corner wash stand, in the hallway, on the stairs – anywhere. He trained seekers, in meditation. By 1895 he was worn out with lecturing and touring across America, always available to all who sought him out. One of his followers offered him the use of a small house at Thousand Island Park, the largest island in the St Lawrence river, and there he stayed with a few American disciples for a while. It was one of the most peaceful, inspired, and illumined oases in his life. Here again he breathed the atmosphere of Dakshineswar; here, he said afterwards, on one occasion, in solitude, he once again experienced Nirvikalpa samadhi. The disciples themselves felt their lives changed. One of them wrote, 'We were taken to the top of Pisgah, and the sorrows and trials of this world have never been quite real since.'

Afterwards he went to England, visiting Paris on the way. He was amazed by the welcome he received in England, and he found the ordinary English people amongst whom for a time he lived, worked and lectured, so different from the 'colonizing sahibs' he had been accustomed to in India, as to seem almost a different species. He wrote that he was delighted to change his opinion of the English: 'My ideas about the English have been revolutionized. They are steady, sincere to the backbone, with great depth of feeling – only with a crust of stoicism on the surface; if that is broken, you get your man.' He visited England twice in this way, and gave some of his finest lectures on yoga (afterwards published) in London, where he became well-known, and popular in the churches and among leading clergymen. From England there came to him some of his greatest Western disciples; Margaret Noble, who followed him to India and became Sister Nivedita, a nun of the Order who, since there was as yet no convent, lived out her life in a house in a back street in Calcutta, teaching Hindu girls, working in plague and famine, inspiring Indian statesmen, scientists, writers and artists to weld India into a living sense of nationalism, and in pride and love for their religion, and all it had to give to the world. Captain and Mrs Sevier also followed him to India and established an ashram in the Himalayas, as a centre for peace and meditation away from the work and activity; and J. J. Goodwin, who became his most faithful disciple until his own early death in India; without him, much of the teaching would have been lost, for he took down the lectures in shorthand for publication. Vivekananda wrote letters all over the world, but he had not enough time for writing books. 'I have no time even to die', he said, though he was a worn and dying man for some years before his own death at the age of thirty-nine.

As well as his world travels, he made two more tours of America, where he was offered a Chair of Eastern Philosophy at Harvard, which he was unable to accept as he was a monk; on one tour he gave over a hundred lectures, and once in a country district stood on a tub in the street to give his talk, while cowboys fired shots round his head to see if his teachings on calmness and self-control were rooted in experience. They found that they were; he continued, unperturbed. His love of people as individuals, his liking for small groups and personal contact, his love of the humblest, never changed. When refused admission to a hotel because it was thought that he was a Negro, he refused to explain that he was a visiting Indian celebrity; he went away. If there was to be a rejection of anyone, he wanted to share it. He founded the Vedanta Society in New York from which eventually sprang the great American Ramakrishna Vedanta Centres which flourish in various parts of America today.

On returning to India, he was welcomed with triumphal arches, flowers, palms, enormous crowds, and his carriage was drawn through the streets in an outburst of sheer joy that came from the heart of a nation which, when it celebrates, celebrates very enthusiastically indeed. Much as he wanted to avoid a personality

Swami Vivekananda

cult, he accepted the joyful welcome that spread across the country, because he knew that India desperately needed a feeling of pride in itself and its religion, a sense that India had something to give to the world; strength and vigour were needed, to overcome apathy and despair.

After more years of work, in which the present monastery of the Ramakrishna Order was established at Belur, and a temple built to Ramakrishna, the work of serving the needy began in plague and famine, sick-nursing, the care of homeless children; it was all beginning, and helpers began to come forward with money or offering practical assistance as lay workers. At first, the orthodox were horrified to see Brahmins touching 'unclean' lepers; just as the orthodox in the West had been horrified to see time 'wasted' in meditation, and equal acceptance given to all religions. To those who could only stay at home and live their own domestic lives, he was always encouraging; this was their duty, this was as important as great humanitarian work.

As I grow older, I find that I look more and more for greatness in little things. I want to know what a great man eats and wears, and how he speaks to his servants. More and more the true greatness seems to me that of the worm, doing its duty silently, steadily, from moment to moment, and hour to hour.

Two years before he died, he wrote a letter to a friend:

The battles are lost and won. I have bundled my things and am waiting for the great deliverer. After all, Joe, I am only the boy who used to listen with rapt wonderment to the wonderful words of Ramakrishna under the Banyan at Dakshineswar. That is my true nature; works and activities, doing good and so on, are all impositions. Now I again hear his voice; the same old voice, thrilling my soul. Bonds are breaking, love dying, work becoming tasteless – the glamour is off life. Only the voice of the Master calling . . . 'I come, my beloved Lord, I come.' I am glad I was born, glad I suffered so, glad I did make big blunders, glad to enter peace. I leave none bound, I take no bonds. . . . Oh, Joe, The blessedness of it! Everything is good and beautiful; for things are all losing their relative proportions to me – my body among the first. 'OM' That Existence!

He had always taught that the soul neither comes nor goes, it eternally *is*; work, service, all the noblest things in life which he regarded as vital, were nevertheless 'imposed' for a time on 'That Existence' for the burning away of dross, for the purification of

a

the soul, to prepare it for the Highest. He was ready to go; but he had said again and again that he would face a thousand lives of reincarnation if he could serve even one human life which needed him.

On Friday, 4 July 1902, the day of American Independence, Vivekananda died. He had always said that death was the moment of glorious independence, when the body fell away but the soul stood, as it had always in fact been, perfect in its own existence. He had seemed so well that his brother monks rejoiced that his many illnesses seemed momentarily better. In the morning he closed all doors and windows, which he had never done before, and meditated quite alone by the shrine of Ramakrishna in the Belur monastery. At lunch he laughed and joked with the novices; in the afternoon he gave three hours of instruction to them on Sanskrit grammar, interspersed with jokes and stories; he took a walk with a brother monk; in the evening, he meditated alone in his room. He entered meditation with a serene and radiant expression; and he never returned.

Three days before he died, he had pointed to a corner of the monastery grounds, and said, 'When my time comes, cremate me there'. This was done, and all Calcutta, stunned with grief, poured in, to the cremation. Today a temple stands on the place of cremation.

Vivekananda had said : 'It may be that I shall find it good to get outside my body – to cast it off like a worn-out garment. But I shall not cease to work. I shall inspire men everywhere until the world shall know that it is one with God.'

Neither he nor his Master offered a dogma, an easy cure-all to be taken like medicine. They sounded a harmony which can still be heard today.

3

THE CHAOS

What is chaos?

A heartfelt, if ungrammatical, answer might be given to that question : 'Chaos is what we live in a time of.' But that is an answer which might equally well have been given during any period of history, back to the beginnings of recorded time. Possibly today the worried awareness of chaos is increased by the media, especially television, which brings world chaos only too vividly into our own homes, but the increase is less in the chaos than in our awareness of it. The next question, 'What is the cause of chaos?' is better not asked at all, unless the questioner has several hours to spare, for the answer will be a very long one and it will in any case be useless as evidence because each one of us will answer the question differently. Your own answer is the correct one. Unless, of course, it differs from mine, in which case it will be the result of prejudice, lack of discernment, and reading the wrong newspapers.

If we avoid falling too deeply into this trap of intolerance, which Ramakrishna in his more teasing moments characterized as 'Everyone's watch tells the wrong time, except mine' (and he would be a brave man who claimed for himself a total freedom from intolerance in all forms and at all times), then we may fall into another trap, just as dangerous. It is a trap less dangerous to the sincere seeker than to the theologian; today, perhaps most dangerous of all to the sociologist or political theorist. It lies in a refusal to consider any question which may upset accepted dogma. Vivekananda, who had a great love and respect for the American Negroes and their stories, was fond of one story about a Negro revivalist preacher, who began his sermon with the words, 'God made man, and then leaned him against the fence to dry.' A questioner immediately interrupted him, 'Who made that fence?' 'One more question like that, brother,' said the harassed preacher, 'and you ruins the whole of theology.'

But the questions must be asked. Ramakrishna insisted on honest questioning. When Vivekananda said, 'I fought my Master for six long years, with the result that I know every inch of the way', he did not mean that there was bitterness or true 'fighting' between them, but a vigorous question and answer, discussion, and argument; a refusal on his part to accept anything which did violence to his reason or his observation, no pretence of doubt when he was truly convinced, no lip-service to pretence of belief when he did not believe, or had not yet experienced.

Obviously, the most vital question of all concerns the chaos within man himself. In playing a symphony, each player can only play his own instrument as perfectly as possible; he cannot play other people's instruments for them, or assert that his is the best, and they should all be playing *his* instrument, in his way. But if he does not trust the sense of harmony within himself, this will deepen his anxiety as to the whole orchestra, and his part in it. He may doubt if the symphony is worth playing, or indeed if it exists at all. Fury or even despair at the performance of the other players add to his own disharmony. And where, in heaven's name, is the conductor?

Our present Age may sometimes seem to us almost too conscious of the chaos within. 'Alienation' has become the fashionable theme for plays, films and books; fragmentation of the mind and character and tragic despair of spirit are best-selling subjects – next to sex, which is the greatest best-seller of all. Modern Existentialist philosophers such as Heidegger, Sartre and Camus have placed their emphasis on angst, anguish and despair. Films and plays concentrate on the grotesque and cruel rather than on the balanced and integrated. This creates a general atmosphere which few can escape. Drug addiction and alcoholism are on the increase; mental hospitals in the West have more beds occupied than hospitals for bodily disease. None of this points to an increase of harmony within. Certainly it adds to the impression of chaos. But it would be a misreading of our life to suggest that there is no brighter side; and it would be very far from the truth to assume that all this leapt upon us overnight, or that wholeness, cheerfulness and harmony existed a few years ago in a serene world, and then were suddenly wiped out by a reign of chaos, as a thriving city might be wiped out by an unexpected earthquake. When Vivekananda visited and stayed in the West in the 1890s, he saw beneath the surface.

He was delighted by the efficiency he found, the organization, the technology, and all that implied, as the social life of the West did, self-discipline, hard work, vitality and vigour. He was impressed by the freedom and spontaneity of Western women, who were unveiled, educated, and as natural in their manner towards him and other men as if they were men themselves; he always delighted in naturalness and lack of self-consciousness. But as he moved freely about America and England, making many friends, staying in their homes and talking to them as individuals, he saw that there was as much suffering in the West as he had seen when he roamed the length of India and was racked by the misery he saw. The suffering was different in kind, and less obvious, but it was there. 'Social life in the West is like a peal of laughter,' he said, 'but underneath it is a wail. It ends on a sob. The fun and frivolity are all on the surface; really, it is full of tragic intensity.'

He might have been speaking today. Clearly, any chaos we see today is no sudden departure from a Golden Age. He began to see that even the life of emancipated women in the West (and he devoted much of his concern to bringing education and a greater degree of freedom and choice to the lives of Indian women) had its own tragedies and difficulties. There were no child-widows, forbidden by custom to marry again, as there were in India, but the lives of unmarried women living in lonely bed-sitting-rooms while they pursued a career in an office was sometimes even lonelier than the life of the Indian widow, who at least lived as a member of a household, with an honoured place in a small community, as a nun. In the greater freedom of sexual choice he saw a possible future in which Western women might lose their dignity and security, when they were no longer honoured as mother-figures and comrades, but might come to be regarded as temporary sex-partners and sex-objects, and so enter a new type of female slavery. In technology, and in political and national efficiency and strength – all of which he admired and struggled to bring to his countrymen – he also saw the seeds of possible future wars and an even more terrible chaos. He accepted all this as inevitable, for his whole philosophy and experience was based on a view of life and the cosmos which accepted the terrible without fear or alarm; all that was conveyed in the Kali-symbol, conveying terror and blessings. He saw the truth beyond all this.

He saw also, very clearly, what was good in the West. He was touched and delighted by the practicality with which human suffering was (sometimes) tackled; he visited a reformatory for

criminals, he rejoiced at the development of orphanages and
hospitals for the poor, and in studying Christianity he was so
deeply impressed by *The Imitation of Christ* that he insisted on a
translation being made for Indians. He studied Christian monastic
systems, and found that in the Middle Ages there had often been
a ceremony at which the head of an order washed the feet of
beggars; in this symbolism, and in the service of the poor and
sick which was often linked with Western monasticism, he saw
something vital for monasticism in India. He read and studied
every philosophy – religious, materialistic, atheistic and psychological – of his day, because he saw that since the advent of
Darwinism and the crumbling of faith in religious dogma, the
West was seeking rationality, and a view of the cosmos which was
capable of standing the test of argument in a scientific era.

He saw that Western despair originated in Western man's
equation of himself with body, mind and personality, instead of
spirit. Obviously, if it is believed that the self depends on the
body for its existence and cannot survive death, or even the loss
of the mind or ego in life, then the problem is entirely one of
identity. 'Come up, O lions,' he said, 'and shake off the delusion
that you are sheep . . . you are not matter, you are not bodies –
matter is your servant, not you the servant of matter.' The
reference to lions and sheep is based on a favourite parable which
expresses the teaching about man's identity. In this parable a
lion cub is orphaned and fostered by a flock of sheep. Naturally,
it grows up thinking itself to be a sheep. A true lion (the guru
or teacher) comes from the jungle, and taking the lion cub to the
pool, forces him to look in and see his true face mirrored; he sees
what he in fact *is*. This, of course, represents meditation. Then
the lion persuades the cub to eat the lion's diet – which is the
selfless living which at first he does not relish – and at last the
two go off together – not to escape life, but to live it fully as befits
a lion. It is significant that there is no suggestion that the lion
cub was wicked; simply, he was living a life of illusion – he had
mistaken his identity.

In India, as opposed to the West, the truths were known, but
had become distorted, or even despised. In his words to his
countrymen he did not spare his much-loved country.

Your religion teaches you that every being is only your own Self
multiplied. But it is the want of practical application, the want of

sympathy, the want of heart. . . . You have the greatest religion the
world ever saw, and you feed the masses with stuff and nonsense.
You have the perennial fountain flowing, and you give them ditch
water.

But in the West he faced the task, as he said, of taking these
great truths, as then largely unknown outside India, and making
of them something which could be grasped with ease and simplicity, but at the same time meet the questionings of the
philosophers; the essence, childlike in its directness, but never
becoming rigidly dogmatic or closed to the philosophy and
thought of any era. 'Out of Yogism must come the most scientific
and practical psychology – and all this must be put in such a form
that a child may grasp it.' He did not underestimate the difficulties.

His first difficulty was to find a name for it. 'Yoga' is usually
taken in the West to apply to Hatha Yoga, the yoga of bodily
control. This is a specialized form of yoga, and not one advocated
by Ramakrishna, who felt that it put too much emphasis on the
body. Also, it would seem to suggest a sect, a tendency which he
was determined to avoid. How could he find a label for a religion
that was especially directed towards forgetting all labels, and
including them all in one universality? On the other hand, a
title too vague which appeared to approve of everything and
everybody, could quickly degenerate into a 'do as you like, do it
yourself, anything goes' mish-mash which had no strength, no self-
discipline, no central inner pole from which to swing.

'Anta' means 'end of' and the 'Vedas', in particular, are loosely
regarded as that part of the teachings which refer to yoga, that
is, the full experiencing of God. But Vivekananda was giving
the word a new meaning. He said, 'By the Vedas, no books are
meant; the principles, the law of the spirit, the Perennial Philosophy is found in all scriptures to a greater or lesser extent.' Unfortunately, confusion is sometimes caused by the fact that before
the advent of Vivekananda, Vedanta was thought of as a philosophy; one of the six traditional 'darshanas' of Indian philosophy.
It was the name of a special outlook, belonging to the whole
Upanishadic thought, but used as if it were the sole property of
monks, philosophers, hermits or others withdrawn from life.
Vivekananda used it in a new sense; it was to be brought into
practical everyday living with vigour and strength; but the heart
and core of it was the same teaching, the same attitude towards
the identity of man.

This meant that there must be two wings on which the bird flies; one, the universality and the whole philosophy of Vedantic thought; the other, stemming from this and inextricably a part of it, its application in everyday life to each one of us. It is this second wing which we are considering in this book; but before we leave the subject of universality, let us hear what Vivekananda himself had to say about it :

If there is ever to be a universal religion, it must be one which will have no location in space or time; which will be infinite like the God it preaches, and whose sun will fall upon the followers of Krishna and of Christ, on saints and sinners alike; which will not be Brahmanic or Buddhistic or Christian or Mohammedan, but the sum total of all these and still have infinite space for development; which in its catholicity will embrace in its infinite arms, and find a place for every human being from the lowest savage not far removed from the brute, to the highest man towering by the virtues of his head and heart almost above humanity, making society stand in awe of him and doubt his human nature. It will be a religion which will have no place for persecution or intolerance in its philosophy; which will recognize the divinity in every man and woman, and whose whole force will be centred in aiding humanity to realize its own true divine nature.

Turning now to the personal life, that instrument which each one of us plays and whose harmony or disharmony makes our lives fruitful or barren, joyful or despairing. There is in us all a certainty – a conviction – of wholeness, constantly fragmented by fears, anxieties, doubts, desires, frustration, aggression, irritability – as Koko says in *The Mikado* – 'The task of filling in the blanks I'd rather leave to you' – but at our best we know that this is not all that we are. The Ramakrishna/Vivekananda Vedanta speaks to that certainty which knows that somewhere within us, wholeness exists. At our best moments, we express it fully, we find that we are capable of more than we believed possible. In moments of doubt or anguish, or in facing a difficult decision, we know that the note is there, if only we could find it. This very awareness, this longing, this need to live permanently in the strength and certainty that we have already found to be there, when we are 'at our best'; plus a passion for freedom which is beginning to chafe at its bonds; a longing for a love which is not an ephemeral emotion but an enduring reality in which death is only a temporary incident and separation an illusion; a very natural longing for joy, and for true peace; all these, said Rama-krishna, are like the first rays of morning light on the horizon which signal that the sun will soon rise.

There was never any suggestion that this inevitability would lead to an easy time for the seeker. Ramakrishna used many metaphors to underline the truth that life is tough and that great strength is needed (and will be found) especially in the early stages of spiritual life. 'The wind of God's grace is always blowing; but you must unfurl your sail to catch the wind.' He spoke also of the helmsman who had to work to steer his boat against the tide, but later the wind, the change of tide, the bend in the river – all things brought him finally to a place where he had the boat completely in his control and what had been difficult became a natural 'going with the tide'. Metaphors of farmers who worked, sweated, and kept on at the job without pause until it was com-pleted, in spite of terrible harvests and difficulties; of the house-wife who did not go to the Ganges for her evening bathe until all her daily work was done, and then, with a feeling of peace, off she went – 'Then you may call and call after her, but she will not come back'. All these illustrations bring the same idea of something completely natural and inevitable, but needing work and determination. What he stressed – and what Vivekananda poured into all his teachings and all his work – was that, while we have to unfurl the sail, the wind is *there*. The strength comes. It is as truly there, in this world of maya in which we find our-selves, as the blowing of the wind or the rising of the sun.

Even on a purely day-to-day human level, their own lives illustrated their teachings. Ramakrishna reached his spiritual heights after twelve years of lonely and difficult sadhanas. His joy and selflessness remained unchanged throughout an agonizing cancer of the throat; his teachings, which were entirely spoken, needed a voice, and one of his greatest gifts, which people loved to hear, was his singing voice; Vivekananda spoke of his beautiful voice, and there are many references to it. Like the deafness which struck Beethoven at the height of his genius, it seems the one afflic-tion above all others which should *not* have happened to him. Yet, Vedantically speaking, this also means that it gave him the supreme chance to be his true Self, and it made him one with the rest of humanity. How often in our lives have we said, 'I could have coped with anything but *this*'? And 'this' is always the very thing we have to face. Vivekananda's life was mainly lived

out in the world, not behind monastic walls, much as he longed
for solitude. He used his intellectual gifts, his powers of organization, his personal care for every individual who needed him,
under conditions of failing health, while he moved about the
world, and, as he said, 'had not time even to *die*'; but he refused
to be moved one inch from his course, or to lose the fearlessness
which he so constantly preached. The word so often used about
him by people who met him was not 'suffering' but 'blissful' and
frequently, 'loving'. Sarada Devi lived out a life of sweetness,
serenity and dignity, and kept the spiritual greatness for which
she is still literally worshipped, in the midst of problems and
difficulties, travelling, manual work, domestic responsibilities in
her home village, the endless burden of other people's worries;
quietly withdrawn but constantly available to all who came to her
– and they never stopped coming. It is noticeable that the lives
of each of them, and their greatest disciples and followers, all
were lit by that constant touch of humour, of merriment, of deep
and secure joy.

'Truth is One; men call it by many names,' said Ramakrishna.
The truth of any teachings must stand the test of daily living,
however difficult the conditions, whatever the changes in current
values, outlook, or fashions in living.

4

IS GOD A PERSON?

The difficulties which Vivekananda faced in giving to Western countries the spiritual teachings he longed to share, were considerable. He was frank about the problems in his letters and discussions. The doubts set moving by Darwinism were turning seekers away from devotion to a personal God. The worship of Jesus Christ as a personality had often become insipid, 'churchianity' rather than true Christianity, and sincere thinkers were distressed or doubting. At the other end of the spectrum stood the very narrow, rigid and dogmatic sects of the churches. Many Westerners agreed with him when he found it difficult to equate the purity, poverty and self-abnegation of Jesus with a civilization so affluent, and so ready to rely on the army and on trade, in relationships with countries overseas. On the other hand, educated Westerners were insisting on intellectual conviction. They expected him to put into words heights of spirituality for which there are no words; they wanted clear-cut definition. In one sense, he sympathized with them. He himself had always refused to go one inch beyond what his reason could accept; no spiritual teaching should do violence to reason, he believed. He would not ask them to go beyond reason in the early stages; but it could hardly take them the whole way. Also, they had not experienced his own spiritual states. And they had not watched Ramakrishna, listened to him, seen the living evidence.

Another problem lay in the urgency of the West, with its tensions and anxieties, its belief that this one brief life is all that each of us has, so people expected that spiritual heights must be explained, intellectually accepted, and reached within the span of one lifetime. The gradual unfolding of the soul, which might take many lifetimes in reincarnation to reach final maturity; the absence of haste, without strain or forcing, which still put out full effort – his own thinking was saturated with this. But his own Westernized education in Calcutta had helped him to understand the difficulties, and the teaching of Ramakrishna – that the teacher must learn to stand where the student stands, almost to become the student in his sympathies if he is to help him – proved its wisdom again and again when Vivekananda spoke to the West.

Another problem he had to face was the Western belief that good and evil, joy and suffering, known to Vedanta as 'the pairs of opposites', are regarded in the West as being distinct and separate from each other, and evil thus appears to be something which God, as it were, permitted but regretted. He had dedicated himself to a refusal to destroy the faith of any human soul; he treated with the utmost delicacy the established beliefs of those who came to him, and it was said of him that he seemed to regard it almost as a blasphemy to intrude, unasked, into the spiritual lives of those he met. But people flocked to him who were obviously starving for the truth which they believed that he was himself experiencing and living. They were weary of teachers who could draw detailed spiritual maps for them, but who only too clearly did not inhabit the country they described.

His English disciple, Margaret Noble, who followed him to India and adopted both the country and its religion, living and dying there as a nun, said of him when she first met him in England :

It was his *character* to which I had thus done obeisance. As a religious teacher I saw that although he had a system of thought to offer, nothing in that system would claim him for a moment, if he found that truth led elsewhere. . . . For the rest, I studied his teachings sufficiently to become convinced of their coherence, but never, till I had had experiences which authenticated them, did I inwardly cast in my lot with the final justification of the things he came to say.

This had been his own attitude. To be drawn towards truth; to listen, to long for certainty, even, sometimes, to be hard to convince – and then, if possible, to experience. He much preferred this to a sentimental excitement in his audiences for exotic Oriental ideas, or, at the other extreme, to arid intellectualism which could write a thesis on the subject, but which lacked the fervent depth of a simple peasant with her rosary.

In addressing audiences, he gave the philosophy on which all was based, 'the shining, the strengthening, the bright philosophy' as he called it. He made it clear that he was giving the great truth which, he believed, underlies all religions. He never attempted to convert his audience to any specific religion, or any sect. He told them that the scriptures of Hinduism, the Vedas, like all scriptures, were needed by the aspirant in the early stages. But he went on to say :

Of all the scriptures of the world, it is the Vedas alone which declare that the study of the Vedas is secondary . . . 'I reject the Vedas !' is the last word of the Vedanta philosophy. . . . Personally, I take as much of the Vedas as agrees with reason.

He was echoing the teaching of Ramakrishna, and of Hindu teachers throughout the ages, that when a friend has sent a letter of instructions, one keeps it and studies it until all the instructions have been carried out, and then one can tear it up. Instructions can only go so far.

We admit the imperfection of our system, because the reality must be beyond all systems; and in this admission lies the promise and portent of an eternal growth. Sects, ceremonies and books, so far as they are the means of a man's realizing his own nature, are all right. When he has realized *that*, he gives up everything.

Then he went on to give the philosophy, the world-view of the cosmos, and of all that we know and see; beginning at the peak and then showing the various paths. In this form of presentation there is the difficulty of names. 'God' is a word capable of many interpretations, though he always came back to it, as it is a name so familiar and so beloved to many people. 'The Lord', as applied to the Absolute, may suggest a person; the words 'That' or 'The Absolute' or 'The Impersonal' sound cold and remote. So he used the name of The Ultimate, as it is used in India : Brahman.

Brahman, Ramakrishna had said, has never been defiled by the lips of man, for It cannot be described or defined. Sometimes, in his longing to help his disciples, Ramakrishna described to them the various stages of his experience as he entered the state of samadhi; but always he reached a state of 'becoming' where he could not speak, where words could no longer describe the experience. Later he wept, and assured them that he would have described it to them if he could. But how can you describe colour to one as yet blind, without giving him the faculty of sight ? It was to the development of this spiritual faculty to which a lifetime – perhaps many reincarnations – should be given. But some words must be used, so Vivekananda, in the West, explained that Brahman, though It cannot be described, is Being; the Ultimate; pure Existence – Knowledge – Bliss (Satchidananda); remaining from eternity to eternity; the ultimate Reality.

Brahman is not a state. It is the only unit composed of many units. It is the principle that runs through all, from a cell to God, without which nothing can exist. Whatever is real is that principle or Brahman.

Brahman is actionless. But the power of Brahman, the primal energy, is often called 'maya' (Avidya, Prakriti, Sakti) – the names are many but Vivekananda used the word 'maya' to describe the whole universe as we know it. Brahman is the Being, maya is the Becoming; like a snake lying still, and the same snake when it moves. The kali image in the temple at Dakshineswar depicts Shiva as the Absolute, lying still. Kali is projected from him. She is beautiful and hideous, cruel and kind, good and bad, the 'pairs of opposites'. She resolves all paradoxes; she is everything we find in ourselves. Kali dances.

Another word which he used constantly in this connection, was 'Atman'. This is the individual Soul, which is one with the supreme soul; the essence; our own true 'essence of Brahman', as a river is one with the ocean. This remains unchanged throughout all the reincarnations which an individual soul may experience. When a belief in reincarnation is not accepted, it makes no difference to the teaching concerning the Atman; the individual soul is in reality That. The parable which illustrates this, tells of the busy bird hopping up and down on the branches of the tree of life, tasting sweet and bitter fruits, until at last he realizes that the serene, golden, unchanging bird which remains in eternal stillness at the top of the tree is in fact his own true Self.

The one question which Vedanta does not answer, is the question, 'Why?' When Vivekananda was asked *why* Brahman projected the 'illusion', the 'magic' of maya – the pair of opposites, the universe – he always replied that while we are still caught within maya, the question cannot be answered, for as yet we are not ready; the intellect which answers questions is also bound in maya. And once we have 'become', then the question, the questioner, and the answer, will no longer exist for us.

The religions of the world, he explained, give different approaches to the ultimate Reality, and these approaches are not as contradictory as they appear, but complementary and suited to different temperaments, and sometimes to different nations.

The Upanishads told 5000 years ago that the realization of God could never be had through the senses. So far, modern agnosticism agrees, but the Vedas go further than the negative side and assert in the plainest terms that man can and does transcend this sense-bound universe. He can, as it were, find a hole in the ice through which he can pass and reach the whole ocean of life. . . . We cannot *know* Brahman, but we *are* Brahman. . . . The apparent variety is but the reflection seen in time and space, as we see the sun reflected in a million dew-drops.

He was speaking of the heights of Non-Dualism (Monism) in which the seeker, called a 'jnani' as he follows the path of Jnana Yoga, cuts everything from him and gives his life to seeking a full realization of the illusory nature of maya, and of all things that we see. The jnani struggles to find his total oneness with all, by first rejecting all, in order to find his true Self and live in It. This is the toughest path of all in many ways, and few are the souls who are ready for it in its complete form, or whose duties in the world make it possible, but he set it out for his listeners in terms of the highest philosophy before he went on to the difficulties and practicalities.

Man is *not* bound by the law of causation. Pain and misery are not man, he is never born, he does not die, he is not in time and space. These ideas are mere reflections of the mind, but we mistake them for reality and so lose sight of the glorious truth they obscure. Time is but the method of our thinking, but we are the eternally present tense. Only by going to the Centre, by unifying ourselves with God, can we escape the delusion of the senses. . . . The satisfaction of desire only increases it, as oil poured on fire but makes it burn more fiercely. The further from the Centre, the faster goes the wheel, the less there is rest. Draw near the Centre, check desire, stamp it out, let the false self go, then our vision will clear and we shall see God.

In fact, he taught, the soul neither comes nor goes, it eternally *is*. As we read a book and turn the pages, we seem to be living through the experiences we encounter in the story, but it is the pages that turn, the story that goes forward; we remain where we are, only apparently involved. Lives and deaths in reincarnation are only the turning of many pages; the witnessing soul watches.

Both happiness and misery are chains, the one golden, the other iron, but both are equally strong to bind us and hold us back from realizing our true nature. The Atman knows neither happiness nor misery. These are merely 'states' and states must ever change. The nature of the soul is bliss and peace unchanging. We have not to *get* it; we have it. Let us wash away the dross from our eyes and see it. We must stand ever on the Self and look with perfect calmness upon all the panorama of the world.

The jnani follows the path of discrimination; he thinks in terms of the Ultimate; he is not concerned with personal God, whom he regards as the Ultimate seen through the mists of the senses, and he is cutting the senses and all that he sees and feels, away from him. It is a swifter path than the slower and more natural path of love, of devotion to a personal God, but it has its dangers. It is an austere and isolated path, 'wandering alone, like the wind' and though it attracts the philosopher and the man of knowledge, it is very difficult to combine it, in its full and 'specialized' form, with a life in the world, with all life's duties and entanglements. It contains the danger of dryness, of aridity, or intellectualism. To say 'I am That' is downright dangerous when the 'I' is still equated with the ego and the body. It is only the man who has achieved control of his own ego and has experienced his own complete separation from body and mind, who can truly say, 'I am That'. Yet this superb path beckons to us all, as it has beckoned to seekers through the ages.

The great question to which Vivekananda led his audiences, was the question of the achievement of universal consciousness; can this also be achieved by the path of Bhakti, the devotion to a personal God? Ramakrishna had fully demonstrated in his life the possibility of a harmony between the yogas. But whether there is to be a harmony within the seeker himself, with one nature or approach predominating, or whether one path is to be followed totally; whether the seeker is a jnani, following the path of discrimination, or a bhakta, following completely the path of acceptance, of worship of a personal God; in both cases, there must be the utter simplicity of the child-nature. Without that, the achievement of universal consciousness is not possible.

A young child has no difficulty in feeling that everything is filled with consciousness. If we watch a very tiny child who is just beginning to walk and explore the world, he will touch a velvet cushion in delighted discovery of this new thing called 'texture'. Then he will touch his own skin, and find that it is different. He is learning that he is separate, distinct from other things; and so he must, on a practical level; unfortunately, the older he grows, the greater will the separation become, until it becomes spiritual as well.

As Vedanta teaches, and as Vivekananda often said, we have become hypnotized by maya into thinking in terms of separate individuals and things, of regarding the One as many. Those who meditate are sometimes accused of self-hypnotization. In fact, meditation is a process of de-hypnotization. We must behave as though there are many, all separated; or life could not go on. We have to go forward to that state of simplicity which the child gradually lost; but now the adult is aware of a universal consciousness behind the apparent separation.

Thomas Traherne, the seventeenth-century poet and mystic, speaking of his own childhood, wrote :

My knowledge was Divine; I knew by intuition those things which since my apostasy I collected again by the highest reason. My very ignorance was advantageous. . . . Everything was at rest, free, and immortal. All Time was Eternity . . . I knew no churlish proprieties, nor bounds nor divisions . . . with much ado I was corrupted, and made to learn the dirty devices of this world, which now I unlearn, and become, as it were, a little child again, that I may enter into the Kingdom of God.

In those words he gives us the Vedantic atmosphere; the pure air. The words known the world over – Wordsworth's 'Heaven lies about us in our infancy/ Shades of the prison-house begin to close/ Upon the growing boy' – are all too often taken out of the context of the title of the poem, 'Intimations of Immortality'. The words mean exactly what they say.

In a charming incident, and with his usual simplicity, Ramakrishna gave the same great truth, when visiting the house of a devotee. Ramakrishna left the room without noticing that a little girl, six or seven years old, had saluted him in the full Hindu obeisance to indicate respect. On his return she said to him indignantly, 'I saluted you, and you didn't even notice it !' She then insisted on saluting him again – 'The other foot, too,' she said, and Ramakrishna then returned the salute, bowing to the child and touching the ground with his forehead. Then he gathered the child and her little friends around him, and 'sang light and frivolous songs to entertain them'.

He was very happy with the children, and told the adults

D

afterwards that a Paramahamsa (a great soul who has reached a high state of illumination) is like a five-year-old child.

He sees everything filled with Consciousness. At one time I was staying at Kamarpukur when Shivaram [his nephew] was four or five years old. One day he was trying to catch grasshoppers near the pond. The leaves were moving. To stop their rustling he said to the leaves: 'Hush! Hush! I want to catch a grasshopper.' Another day it was stormy. It rained hard. Shivaram was with me inside the house. There were flashes of lightning. He wanted to go out. I scolded him and stopped him, but still he peeped out now and then. When he saw the lightning, he exclaimed, 'There, uncle! They are striking matches again!' The Paramahamsa is like a child.

So, with childlike simplicity, the jnani and the bhakta move towards the experience of universal consciousness. The jnani takes the path of discrimination and cuts free of all entanglements; his goal is Freedom. He will eventually reach a state where he goes beyond even feeling that he is 'a part' of the Ultimate, but finds the whole of it within himself. He sees the whole world as a dream, imposed for a time on ultimate Reality.

But, as Ramakrishna pointed out, it is all very well to assert that 'I am That' and the world is a dream – up to the point when a thorn pierces your foot. As long as the seeker is still identifying himself with his body and ego, as long as he has many duties to perform in the world, and especially if his nature is a loving and perhaps emotional one, then the path of Bhakti, the way of devotion and love, the worship of a personal God, may be a wiser path for him. In his own words:

It is the unwavering conviction of the jnani that Brahman alone is real, and the world illusory. All those names and forms are illusory, like a dream. What Brahman is, cannot be described. But the bhaktas accept all the states of consciousness, they take the waking state to be real also. . . . They say God is within us, in our hearts. Again, he is outside. The most advanced devotees [bhaktas] say that He Himself has become all this – the 24 cosmic principles, the universe and all living beings. The devotee of God wants to eat sugar, not to become sugar.

The illustration of eating sugar, not becoming sugar, is a vividly simple rendering of the distinction between the somewhat academic words, 'Dualism, Qualified Non-Dualism, and Non-Dualism (Monism)'. In Dualism, the bhakta worships a God who is at first very far from him; in the early stages of a civilization, he may even worship in fear; certainly in awe. Then he progresses spiritually closer and closer to the personal God, through many stages of love, towards an 'at-oneness' which drives out fear. In Qualified Non-Dualism, as taught by Ramanuja, he is moving towards Non-Dualism and feels that not only is God in his own heart, and manifested in all around him, but that he himself is a part of God, he is strung on God as a pearl is strung on the thread which runs through the entire necklace. The third path, Non-Dualism, goes straight for the Absolute, as we have seen.

In that case, what is meant by 'personal God'? Is this concept only a psychological bromide, a therapy for the mind?

No. As long as we are still bound within our bodies, minds and ego, we must see God through 'the mists of the senses' and as personal. Vivekananda explained:

Ishwara is the sum total of individuals. Yet He Himself is also an individual in the same way as the human body is a unit of which each cell is an individual. Jiva, the soul, and Ishwara, the personal God, are co-existent beings. As long as one exists, the other also must.

Coming even closer still, he explained, personal God is manifested in one whom we call an Incarnation of God. We should not worship him as a man, for that would be idolatry, but as a wave in that ocean of consciousness, for the wave has shape which we can see. While we are still feeling ourselves to be small bubbles, even if made of the same water as the whole ocean, we are carried on the individual wave, or Incarnation, never forgetting that the wave itself is a part of the ocean, as we are.

When we approach Him with the five senses [said Vivekananda, explaining the impossibility of defining or visualizing Brahman] we can only see him as the Personal God. The idea is that the Self cannot be objectified. How can the knower know Himself? But he can cast a shadow, as it were, and the highest form of that shadow, that attempt at objectifying one's Self, is the Personal God.

In speaking of the Incarnation of God, he went on to say:

Talk as you may, try as you may, you cannot think of God but as a man. . . . If the buffaloes desire to worship God, they, in keeping with their own nature, will see him as a huge buffalo; if a fish wishes to worship God, its concept of Him would inevitably be a big fish; and man must think of him as man. Suppose man, the buffalo and

the fish represent so many different vessels; that these vessels all
go to the sea of God to be filled, each according to its shape and
capacity. In man the water takes the shape of man; in the buffalo
the shape of the buffalo; and in the fish the shape of the fish, but
in each of the vessels is the same water of the sea of God. Two
kinds of men do not worship God as man – the human brute who
has no religion [here he does not refer to the atheist, but to a man
very low on the evolutionary ladder, as yet incapable of religion
to any extent, or to one who has deliberately returned to his more
brutal self] and the Paramahamsa who has transcended the limits of
his own human nature.

The Incarnation is here seen as a manifestation, which our
own eyes can recognize, which our own cup can measure. In the
Bhagavad-Gita, Krishna, (God) says, 'Whenever virtue subsides
and irreligion prevails, I create myself for the protection of the
good; for the destruction of all immorality I am coming from
time to time.' This implies a coming of God in many different
Incarnations, to protect the good in man by manifesting it at its
highest point, and sending into the world a wave of spirituality.
Jesus used the words 'I and my father are one' and 'he who has
seen me, has seen the Father' in exactly the same sense. The incarnation does not contain 'the whole of God', but he is that part
of God which our own spiritual vessels can contain. Ramakrishna
sometimes said that one can touch the Ganges at one point, one
does not need to touch the entire Ganges from end to end. It was
said in the First World War that men, terribly wounded in the
trenches, turned to Jesus in their agony precisely because he too
had wounds; they did not want anything remote and beyond
suffering, they wanted a *man*, as Vivekananda said. The famous
poem by Francis Thompson would surely have appealed to
Ramakrishna :

> Yea, in the night, my Soul, my daughter.
> Cry – clinging Heaven by the hems ;
> And lo, Christ walking on the water
> Not of Gennesareth, but Thames.

The phrase, 'Cry – clinging Heaven by the hems' – the idea
of longing, yearning, asking – this was something he emphasized
in all his advice, especially to bhaktas; the restlessness, the yearning, is everything; the child crying for his mother; Ramakrishna
says this again and again.

God with form. . . . Like bubbles rising on a great expanse of water, various divine forms are seen to rise out of the great Akasa of Consciousness. The Incarnation of God is one of these forms. The Primal Energy sports, as it were, through the activities of a divine Incarnation. What is there in mere scholarship? God can be attained by crying to Him, with a longing heart . . .

The answer to the question, 'Is God Personal or Impersonal? What is the *truth*?' was given again and again by Ramakrishna from the experiences he had achieved himself. People came across India to ask him that one question and went away satisfied.

He who is formless is also endowed with form. To his bhaktas he reveals himself as having a form. It is like a great ocean, an infinite expanse of water, without any trace of shore. Here and there some of the water had been frozen. Intense cold has turned it into ice. Just so, under the cooling influence, so to speak, of the bhakta's love, the Infinite appears to take a form. Again, the ice melts when the sun rises; it becomes water as before. Just so, one who follows the path of Knowledge – the path of discrimination – does not see the form of God any more. To him, everything is formless. The ice melts into formless water with the rise of the Sun of Knowledge. But mark this : formlessness and form belong to one and the same Reality.

The word 'Reality' is a very important one; it is always used to mean what is eternal, non-ephemeral. There is no question here of personal God being a convenient psychological way of thinking of the Absolute. The two are one. As long as we are still involved in the world of maya – of personal God, 'Mother' as Ramakrishna saw her, 'Father' to Christians – in whatever form the personal God is regarded – we are still within the realm of Primordial Energy, Primal Consciousness. Personal and Impersonal are not two separate entities, any more than the wave is separate from the sea.

Ramakrishna once said to a disciple,

Nothing whatsoever can be specified about Brahman, except that it exists. Whatever we see or think about is the manifestation of the glory of the Primordial Energy, the Primal Consciousness. Creation, preservation, destruction, living beings and the universe, and further; Bhakti and Prema – all these are manifestations of the glory of that Power. . . . Thinking of the snake, one must think of its wriggling motion, and thinking of the wriggling motion, one must think of the snake.

This Primal Power, Mahamaya, has covered Brahman. As soon as the covering is removed, one realizes 'I am what I was before', 'I am Thou, Thou art I'. But as long as the covering remains, the Vedantic formula, 'I am He', that is, man is the supreme Brahman, does not rightly apply. As long as that covering remains, one should call on God as Mother.

Here he refers to a relationship with Personal God *as* a person – 'Father' to Christians. He went on to speak of the personal relationship with the personal God, as child to parent, parent to child, servant to master, friend to friend, beloved to beloved. 'I know that God is both with and without form. And He may have many more aspects. It is possible for Him to be everything.'

In the West, Vivekananda found a delighted response to this teaching of the ultimate greatness latent in each soul, and of its at-oneness with others. His Western disciples noted that he always spoke to what was finest in each person he met; he made no concessions to fear, weakness, timidity or self-doubts; and instinctively they reacted by meeting him at their highest point. We are all happiest when we are at our best, not at war with ourselves.

He gave the full Vedantic teaching, but he found, as Rama-krishna had said, that few who are inevitably tangled in the world can go beyond the great consciousness of being at one with God : Ramanuja's doctrine of Qualified Non-Dualism. And this he saw as certainly a vital step on the way to the final attainment, and a beautiful path in its own right. So, he showed the gradual progress from the soul completely separated from God in the very earliest stages of Dualism. He showed them the heights, then paid loving acknowledgement to the full heights of Bhakti, which was equally a path to the Ultimate. He took each aspirant exactly as he was, encouraging him to follow the leading of his own inner nature along its natural path. But he showed them the doctrine of Non-Dualism first : 'Tie the Non-Dual knowledge in the corner of your garment, and then follow your own path.'

Of the personal-impersonal views of God, he quoted as Rama-krishna had often done. Hanuman, best of the jnanis, said to Rama (God), 'When I think of myself as the body, then I am Thy servant; when I think of myself as an individual soul then I am Thy part; and when I think of myself as the Atman, then I am Thyself.' This gives with the utmost simplicity the heart of the complex-sounding, 'Dualism, Qualified Non-Dualism, and Non-Dualism'.

Great jnani that he was, Vivekananda was also, as he said, 'bhakta within', just as Ramakrishna had been in Vivekananda's view, 'bhakta without, jnani within'. This great balance was always felt by those who knew them both. As far as the yogas were concerned, and the question of 'God Personal or Impersonal?' each of the two men was his own best illustration. Neither made great claims for himself, both were indifferent to success or failure, both taught others when they were asked, but they were concerned to *be,* and help others to be.

But when minds hunger, truths must be spoken, words must be used. Words are a tool, said Vivekananda, but they are not yoga. Vedanta is not words, it is not theorizing; and Yoga of any kind is not just a therapy. His doctrine of Advaita Vedanta included all the yogas and all religions, but it included them in a harmony. There must be nothing vague or unclear, he insisted, nothing facile or sentimental; and no longing to acquire psychic powers, for these are a hindrance on the path. The philosophy and experience will be clear, shining, strengthening, compassionate, joyful – but these are only words, until they are experienced. In particular, there must be no taking of words and making a cult out of them, to throw at other cults. In talking of the yogas, he went straight to the heart of the matter, and he warned them of the danger of words without the spirit which alone gives life to the words.

Is it possible that there should ever reign unbroken harmony in this plane of mighty religious struggle? The world is exercised in the latter part of this century by the question of harmony; in society, various plans are proposed, and attempts are made to carry them into practice; but we know how difficult it is to do so. People find that it is almost impossible to mitigate the fury of the struggle of life, to tone down the tremendous nervous tension that is in man. Now, if it is so difficult to bring harmony and peace to the physical plane of life – the external, gross, and outward side of it – then a thousand times more difficult is it to bring peace and harmony to rule over the internal nature of man. I would ask you for the time being to come out of the network of words. . . . There is no other teacher to you than your own soul. Recognize this. What comes of it? In society there are so many different natures. There are thousands and thousands of varieties of minds and inclinations. A thorough generalization of them is impossible, but for our practical purpose, it is sufficient to have them characterized into four classes.

The four classes are the four great yogas. In them, alienation and chaos in the psyche of man, or in the world outside, can find healing and certainty. Like the lost lion cub, man can discover his true nature. In his consideration of the yogas, Vivekananda, like his Master before him, was extremely practical.

5

JNANA YOGA: THE YOGA OF KNOWLEDGE

Vivekananda, in addressing audiences, especially in the West where religious and philosophical ideas were in a state of flux and doubt, gave the full philosophy in its simplest terms, so that his audiences could examine the ideas intellectually and in the light of experience. A reasoned approach was their great need; no dogma, no flat assertion. The reaction of his disciple Margaret Noble (afterwards, in her life in India, known as Sister Nivedita) when she first heard him speak in London was not an immediate intellectual conviction. She thought about his teaching for many months and returned to it again and again. Later, she wrote : 'The feeling that great music wakes in us, grows and deepens by its repetition.' She heard the note and it awakened in her something which had struggled for years to come to terms with the poverty and suffering she saw around her, until her belief in a fatherly God who was entirely benevolent and kind, as we understand the words, did violence to her reason.

Years later, travelling with Vivekananda in the Himalayas, she spoke to a young monk, a disciple of Vivekananda, who had been through exactly her own doubts about the nature of God, and she began to see that in India, as well as the West, the differing approaches to religious thinking could clash within the mind of the seeker, and she began to hear the notes of harmony under the apparent tragedy and chaos. She wanted to look life full in the face, without backing away from what she saw there; and so did the monk, Swami Swarupananda, of whom she later wrote :

The story of his mental development was of extraordinary interest to me. For this man had been brought up in his childhood in the Vaishnava faith, that is to say, the idea of God as the kind and loving Lord and preserver of men, which is practically tantamount to the Christianity of the West. The usual revulsion, familiar to all of us, had been encountered. . . . Passing through a crowded street one day, he found a poor woman kneeling and crying softly, as grain by grain she picked up from the dust a handful of rice that had been jostled out of the bowl in her hand by a passer-by. And then the man found himself, in his passionate pity, crying indignantly, 'What the devil would God be doing, if He existed, to let such things happen?'

Two or three such experiences precipitated him upon a year of mental suffering so keen that he never again knew perfect health. But he emerged from it in the peace that comes of a settled attitude towards life. *He would break the dream.* He saw in the ignorance and selfishness of the mind itself the source of such things, and he determined to reach the point of utmost insight and certainty. Under his influence I began seriously the attempt at meditation.

She had no idea then that she would in time become an Indian national figure; the Indian postage stamp that was recently issued in her honour would have seemed unbelievable to her at that time. Others heard Vivekananda, and their lives were changed in totally different directions. Whether they were heading for marriage, monasticism, a career, or the continuation of life exactly as before, slowly the focus changed and deepened. He did not strive for conversion; he was 'calling the sleeping lion to awake' in each person. They took as much or as little of what he had to give, as each one needed.

The teaching or advice of Ramakrishna, though it led to the same harmony, was given in very different circumstances. He did not travel about the world, he remained in his room and people came to him as individuals, and on occasion he visited their houses. As his fame began to spread, and crowds might have gathered, he died. It might be said that he was the heart, the withdrawn inner fire from which sprang Vivekananda's energetic and far-reaching work across the world. Also, it often happened that those who came to Ramakrishna had, as Indians, heard almost too much about Non-Dualism (Monism). Some of them were straining after the Absolute although they were still living a worldly life; struggling to combine the great heights of Jnana with the duties of everyday life; convinced that the worship of a personal God or an Incarnation was wrong. They also tended to see the yogas as paths which were totally distinct from each other. Speaking as one who had experienced the heights of Universal Consciousness sought by the jnanis, and also the full experience of Bhakti, the devotion to a personal God, Ramakrishna encouraged each seeker, with an almost loving motherly care, along the path most suited to his own nature.

Vivekananda did the same with individual disciples; but when speaking to audiences he gave the whole picture of the yoga or approach which he was then explaining to them. In considering Jnana Yoga, which he saw as the highest peak of Advaita Vedanta, he did not expect his audience to leap straight into it; he sounded that great note, and then showed how it could lead on to contain within itself all harmonies.

It is illuminating to consider both the teachings of Vivekananda, showing the high peaks in a clearer and more universal form than the West had yet heard, and side by side with his words, the teachings of Ramakrishna, showing how the great Vedantic teachings, familiar though they may have been to many Indians, could – and in some cases should – be taken and used by those still involved in the world and its duties, caught by many tendrils. This led naturally into the teachings of Bhakti Yoga, about which Vivekananda also spoke with the knowledge and love of one who had experienced it.

Vivekananda spoke without notes, speaking straight from his heart to his audience, however vast, however small. His words were taken down on many occasions in shorthand by a disciple and afterwards published. These are his words :

Now, philosophy insists that there is a joy which is absolute, which never changes. That joy cannot be the joys and pleasures we have in this life, and yet Vedanta shows that everything that is joyful in this life is but a particle of that real joy, because that is the only joy there is. Every moment really we are enjoying the absolute bliss, though covered up, misunderstood, and caricatured. Wherever there is any blessing, blissfulness, or joy, even the joy of the thief in stealing, it is that absolute bliss coming out, only it has become obscured, muddled-up, as it were, with all sorts of extraneous conditions, and misunderstood. But to understand that, we have to go through the negation, and then the positive side will begin. We have to give up ignorance and all that is false, and then truth will begin to reveal itself to us. When we have grasped the truth, things which we gave up at first will take new shape and form, will appear to us in a new light, and become deified. They will have become sublimated, and then we shall understand them in their true light . . . we must give them up first, and then we get them back again, deified.

The word which was often called the jewel of Ramakrishna, was 'renunciation'. To Western ears, the word has a cold and arid sound. Some explanation was needed. Renunciation of one's own weaker tendencies simply means 'conquer', or, as Ramakrishna often advised, bring up the opposite tendency; or, in some cases, increase the tendency and then turn it towards God; 'Smear all with God'. If greedy – be greedy for God; if angry, turn anger against whatever holds one back from God – if afraid, be afraid of fear itself (the famous words, 'We have nothing to fear but fear itself' apply well here). In life's relationships, 'renounce' does not mean abandoning one's child and going out to live in the desert; the renunciation here is mental; we renounce the feeling that we *own* the child, or anybody else. We serve God *in* the child and in everything that lives.

The renunciation of the jnani is more swift, immediate and total than the slower but more natural renunciation of the bhakta, who gives up smaller loves as his greater love increases; the lesser loves drop away naturally, as spirituality develops. But to both jnani and bhakta, renunciation of the world means deification of it, in one case by cutting away at a lower level in order to take on again at a higher; in the other, by a slow natural flowering of love. To the bhakta, all things are God's, or are a manifestation of God. To the jnani, all are jnani's own great Self; that is, Brahman. The same shining truth lies in both paths and is the final goal of both natures.

Speaking of Jnana, Vivekananda continues:

As we proceed, we shall find that the ideal of Vedanta is that all wisdom and all purity are in the soul already, dimly expressed or better expressed. . . . The difference between man and man, and in all things in the whole creation, is not in kind but only in degree. The background, the reality of everyone is that same Eternal, Ever-blessed, Ever-pure and Ever-perfect One. It is the Atman, in the saint and the sinner, in men and in animals; it is the same throughout. . . . Thus, the Soul being pure and perfect, the man who does evil is giving the lie unto himself, he does not know the nature of himself. Even in the murderer the pure Soul is there, it dies not. It was his mistake; he could not manifest it; he had covered it up. Nor, in the man who is killed, is the Soul killed. It is eternal. It can never be killed, never destroyed.

In that case, some might ask, why bother to do good at all? Because, Vedanta tells us, as long as we regard ourselves as weak, and behave in an evil – or even in a lazy, mean or selfish way – we are identifying with our small self, with our ego, and with our body and restless brain. So we continue to be chained by desires which only lead to more desires as they become satisfied; always at the mercy of that fear of loss which afflicts us all; as long as we are not living in the strength and peace of the Atman, we are subconsciously increasing nervous tension and inevitable disappointment. We are deluded; like a man living on a diamond mine, playing with glass beads.

Renunciation is the very basis of our true life; every moment of goodness and real life that we enjoy is when we do not think of ourselves. This little separate self must die. Then we shall find that we are in the Real.

Vivekananda explained that the movement of the soul through various reincarnations is as real as the universe is real. When a man 'becomes' in final, full spiritual Realization, the universe (and the movement of the individual lives of the soul) will be seen no more, though it will remain for others.

According to the Advaita philosophy, there is only one thing real in the universe, which is called Brahman; everything else is unreal, manifested and manufactured out of Brahman by the power of maya. To reach back to the Brahman is our goal. We are each one of us that Brahman, that reality, plus this maya. If we can get rid of this maya or ignorance, then we become what we really are.

He saw the difficulties very clearly, and he emphasized that here we walk a razor's edge.

What is meant by giving up desires – how could life go on? It would be suicidal advice, killing the desire and the man too. . . . The solution is this. . . . Have no idea of proprietorship, possessorship. . . . If we understand the giving-up of the world in its old, crude sense, then it would come to this : that we must not work, that we must be idle, sitting like lumps of earth, neither thinking nor doing anything, but must become fatalists, driven about by every circumstance, ordered about by the laws of nature, drifting from place to place. But that is not what is meant. We must work. . . . So, work, says the Vedanta, work incessantly, holding life as something deified, as God Himself.

Which is all very well, says the cynic, but both our experiences and our inheritance in this life, plus possible tendencies brought over from previous lives, if we believe in reincarnation – with all this lumber that we carry around within our own characters, just to say 'All is God' or 'All is That', at our present stage, is really no more than an idea in the head, a certain way of looking at things. We may begin from that, but then what? It is not so easy, when we are up against life in everyday terms.

Vivekananda took the cynic's view sympathetically and dealt with it frankly. He entirely agreed that it was not easy.

It is very easy to talk! From my childhood I have heard of seeing God everywhere and in everything, and then I can really enjoy the world, but as soon as I mix with the world, and get a few blows from it, the idea vanishes. I am walking in the street thinking that God is in every man, and a strong man comes along and gives me a push and I fall flat on the footpath. Then I rise up quickly with clenched fist, the blood has rushed to my head, and the reflection goes. . . . Every religion teaches us to see God in everything and everywhere. Do you not remember in the New Testament how Christ says so? We have all been taught this, but it is when we come to the practical side, that the difficulty begins. . . . Then if such is the case, what is the use of teaching all these things? The use is this, that perseverance will finally conquer. Nothing can be done in a day. . . . And this ideal we must hear about as much as we can, till it enters into our hearts, into our very veins, until it tingles in every drop of our blood and permeates every pore in our body. We must meditate upon it. 'Out of the fullness of the heart the mouth speaketh' and out of the fullness of the heart the hand works, too. It is thought which is the propelling force in us. Fill the mind with the highest thoughts, hear them day after day, think them month after month. Never mind failures, they are quite natural, they are the beauty of life. Where would life be without them?

Vivekananda presented Jnana, the highest and most abstract of all approaches, as being in very truth able to contain within itself, and to encourage, the flowering of many different natures and many different approaches in the creation of a harmony. But he saw, as Ramakrishna did, the possible dangers awaiting the aspirant who was 'jnani only' – a specialist in this approach, as we might say. For centuries in India the path of the jnani had been austere, separate from ordinary living, totally cutting away all maya as illusion; and if it were to be attempted by someone over-optimistic about his spiritual stage of advancement, it is dangerously easy to say 'I am That', and by 'I' to mean the ego, the personality. Such an aspirant could quickly become a petty tyrant, worshipping his own ego. The jnani walks a razor's edge, and Vivekananda said so, frankly. Without the loving humility

of the bhakta, there could be in Jnana a danger of dryness, of
aridity, or, worse still, of a self-deception that the heights had been
reached when they had not. The traps are there; just as the
traps of sentimentality or emotionalism, and of hatred of another
man's god in loving one's own, are traps that lie in wait for the
bhakta.

For a comment on the difficulties, and also an explanation of
the Jnana-nature, and how the world is seen by the jnani, we
can turn to the words of Ramakrishna himself. He was not lecturing in public, as Vivekananda was called upon to do; 'M'
(Mahendranath Gupta) in his book, *The Gospel Of Sri Ramakrishna*, sets out the conversation of Ramakrishna when he was
speaking to individual disciples, devotees, and enquirers. 'M', who
was a headmaster with a Western education, often questioned
him about Jnana. Looking through the eyes of an advanced jnani,
how would one see the world?

Ramakrishna replied:

A jnani sees everything at once – God, maya, the universe, and
living beings. He sees that vidyamaya, avidyamaya, the universe and
all living beings exist and at the same time do not exist. As long
as he is conscious of 'I' he is conscious of 'others' too. Nothing
whatsoever exists after he cuts through the whole thing with the
sword of Jnana. Then even his 'I' becomes as unreal as the magic
of the magician.

Clearly he was describing his own experience in Nirvikalpa
samadhi, and this is a highly advanced state, far beyond that of
the seeker who is still only reasoning and training his mind to
think along these lines. 'M' tells us that as he sat, reflecting on
these words, Ramakrishna continued:

Do you know what it is like? It is as if there were a flower with
twenty-five layers of petals, and you cut them all with one stroke. . . .
You may feel a thousand times that it is all magic, but you are still
under the control of the Divine Mother (maya). You cannot escape
Her. You must do what she makes you do. A man attains brahma-
jnana only when it is given to him by the Divine Mother. Then only
does he see the whole thing as magic; otherwise, not. As long as the
slightest trace of ego remains, one lives within the jurisdiction of the
Adyasakti.

This danger of self-delusion in no way detracted from his teachings about the beauty of the ultimate heights. He made it clear,
again and again, that if the seeker is a jnani *only* – a specialist,

rather than one who makes a harmony of that and other aspects of his spiritual nature – then it is very difficult, if not impossible, for him to remain involved in worldly duties, or to run an organization. On one occasion, talking about his own earlier experiences, he said,

Formerly I had the state of mind of a jnani; I couldn't enjoy the company of men . . . everything seemed to me impermanent, so I couldn't enjoy people's company. Later the Mother brought my mind down to a lower plane. She so changed my mind that I could enjoy the love of God and His devotees.

Ramakrishna said many times that the man who has reached the roof, sees that the roof and the steps leading to the roof are all made of the same material – it is all One; which brings us back to the Vedantic viewpoint as always. But this is not the same thing as saying that, since it is all one, the soul can leap straight into infinity – straight to the roof from the ground floor. Ramakrishna said :

How can you be a jnani if you are conscious of disease, grief, pain, pleasure and the like? A thorn enters your flesh, blood flows from the wound, and you suffer very badly from the pain; but never the less if you are a jnani, you must be able to say, 'Why, there is no thorn in my flesh at all. Nothing is the matter with me.'

Ramakrishna taught sometimes the harmony of Vijnana, by which, after attaining Knowledge of the Absolute, one affirms the universe and sees it as the manifestation of Brahman. Once the whole picture was seen, as Vivekananda also taught, then the Yoga of Love and Devotion (Bhakti) and indeed all possible paths, began to shine more clearly for his listeners as being a part of the whole Vedantic harmony.

The jnani gives up his identification with worldly things, discriminating, 'Not this, not this' – only then can he realize Brahman. It is like reaching the roof of a house by leaving the steps behind, one by one. But the Vijnani, who is more intimately acquainted with Brahman, realizes something more. He realizes that the steps are made of the same materials as the roof : bricks, lime, and brick-dust. That which is realized intuitively as Brahman, through the eliminating process of 'not this, not this', is then found to have become the universe and all its living beings. The Vijnani sees that the reality which is without attributes, is also with attributes. A man cannot live on the roof a long time. He comes down again. . . . The man coming down from Samadhi perceives that it is Brahman who has become the universe, the ego and all living beings. The path of Knowledge, Jnana, leads to Truth, as does the path that combines Knowledge and Love. The path of Love, Bhakti, too, leads to the goal. The way of Love is as true as the way of Knowledge. All paths ultimately lead to the same Truth. But as long as God keeps the feeling of ego in us, it is easier to follow the path of Love.

Vivekananda, in his lectures on Jnana Yoga in the West, was equally practical, warning against too much *talk* about 'universal brotherhood and equality'. Those who really have it, as he pointed out,

do not make little sects for universal brotherhood, but their acts, their movements, their whole life, show out clearly that they in truth possess the feeling of brotherhood . . . they do not speak, they *do*, and they live. . . . At the centre, where all the radii meet, all our differences will cease, but until we reach there, differences there must be. . . . Each of us is naturally growing and developing according to his own nature, each will in time come to know the highest truth.

So the bhakta is moving to the same point as the jnani; as a consideration of the Yoga of Love and Devotion – Bhakti – will show us.

6

BHAKTI YOGA: THE YOGA OF LOVE AND DEVOTION

The ultimate experience of Bhakti Yoga, as in Jnana and indeed all the yogas, cannot be described, and Ramakrishna did not attempt to do so. The words 'love' and 'devotion' are so often sentimentalized that they are inadequate to describe a state which finally passes beyond emotion as we understand it, to the experience of a Primal Force, and ultimately beyond that. To play with fine-sounding terms remains simply an intellectual exercise, so Ramakrishna spoke in simple, forthright human terms, as he always did, putting aside anything that might sound esoteric or out-of-reach. He spoke always of the steps that were necessary once the first glimmerings had awakened. He was often speaking to beginners, sometimes to the more advanced, and sometimes to those in whom there was no more than a longing for something which they instinctively felt to be there, but which they could not achieve. Some who came to him expected him to tell them that they must belong to a certain sect, or adopt certain disciplines, follow elaborate rituals, or read the holy books, before the first step could be taken. The words 'It is simpler than that!' shone out of everything he said. As with all the yogas, he taught that complete sincerity and childlike simplicity were as necessary to the great scholars who came to him, as they were to the uneducated. Statesmen, writers, dramatists, scientists, musicians, students, monks, housewives, and those who could not write their own name – they all received the same advice as regards essentials. It is advice familiar to Christians; for Christianity is a religion of Bhakti.

God cannot be realized by a mind that is hypocritical, calculating, or argumentative. One must have faith and sincerity. Hypocrisy will not do. To the sincere, God is very near; but He is far, far away from the hypocrite.

One must have for God the yearning of a child. The child sees nothing but confusion when his mother is away. You may try to cajole him by putting sweetmeats in his hand; but he will not be fooled. He only says, 'No, I want to go to my mother.' One must feel such yearning for God. Ah, what yearning! How restless a child feels for his mother! Nothing can make him forget his mother. He to whom the enjoyment of worldly happiness appears tasteless, he who takes no delight in anything of the world – money, name, creature-comforts, sense-pleasure – becomes sincerely grief-stricken for the vision of the Mother. And to him alone the Mother comes running, leaving all her other duties.

This, as his listeners knew, described a very high state of spiritual advancement; many of them were still in the state of the 'bird hopping on the tree of life' tasting its sweet and bitter fruits, and only occasionally longing to draw nearer to that golden bird on the top of the tree. To them, in the same homely metaphor, he explained that the mother would know that the child was happy, playing with its toy; but sooner or later the cry 'I want my mother!' would begin, and it was then that the mother ran to take the child in her arms. That very restlessness – the feeling that a life spent playing with toys is not enough, that a greater security is needed, and a more all-inclusive love – that is the first stirring, the first beginning. As with Jnana Yoga, few leap straight into sainthood in one jump.

Ah, that restlessness is the whole thing. Whatever path you follow – whether you are a Hindu, a Mussalman, a Christian, a Sakta, a Vaishnava, or a Brahmo – the vital point is restlessness. God is our Inner Guide. It doesn't matter if you take a wrong path – only you must be restless for Him. He Himself will put you on the right path.

The first stirring – that restless longing for something that the world could not give – was the important sign.

'At the approach of dawn the eastern horizon becomes red. Then one knows it will soon be sunrise. Likewise if you see a person restless for God, you can be pretty certain that he hasn't long to wait for His vision.' He gave advice on daily living to those who were bhaktas, but still very much involved in the world. The advice was practical and simply given and we will return to it in a later chapter. But in the West Vivekananda had first to explain what Bhakti Yoga *is*. The words 'God is love' can be a convenient bromide, a text to hang on the wall, or they can be the inner power and security of a whole life.

The pathway is not taken alone. Just as in Jnana Yoga it was stressed that man is not an isolated puddle, but behind him is

the infinite ocean of Blessedness, ready to flood in; so in Bhakti
Yoga, once the first steps are taken – when the child 'calls to
mother' as Ramakrishna said – the mother comes running. Sometimes, said Ramakrishna, God attracts the devotee; sometimes
God is attracted by the devotee. In Ramanuja's commentary,
quoted by Vivekananda: 'so that this beloved [devotee] may
attain the Atman the Lord himself helps. For it has been said
by the Lord: "Those who are constantly attached to Me and
worship Me with love – I give that direction to their will by which
they come to me." '

There are two stages in Bhakti; the earlier, or preparatory
stage, and the ripe stage, called the supreme stage. It is in the
earlier stages, whether in an individual or in a whole civilization
which is still at a primitive stage, that the hideous fanaticism
occurs which has so often stained the history of religion with
blood. The fanatics of all the major world religions have always
been at that earlier, preparatory stage where loyalty to Ishwara
(personal God) can lead to torture, war or persecution of those
who worship some other form of God. It is a natural reaction and
perhaps even an inevitable one at a very early stage where love
is defensive or aggressive against anybody outside the chosen fold;
Hell is promised for 'outsiders' in the next world, and frequently
ensured for them in this one. In primitive societies, a God of
wrath and vengeance may seem almost a necessity; man will
objectify his own highest ideal and worship it. At this stage, he
will also feel that God is far away from him and the meticulous
performance of rites assumes great importance. There is often
much beauty in this earlier stage, and great devotion; wonderful
mythologies, colour and art may spring from it. But exclusiveness
and a pride in ritual rather than ethics or spirituality are the
dangers which may hold back a soul, or poison a religion, at this
stage; and sometimes there may be a facile sentimentality, a
feeling of 'God is looking after me, so why should I bother?'
which takes away the great inner strength which is needed on any
spiritual path. Vivekananda said, 'I preach *strength*', and Ramakrishna disliked any approach which he called 'mushy, lacking in
grit'. The pitfalls are obvious; but in the preparatory stage many
concrete supports are needed to help the bhakta progress.
Spiritual giants have nearly all arisen from religions which are
rich in mythology and ritualism; and there are many people who
need an outward form of worship, something to *do*. But in the

end, we find that this is not enough. All these things – rituals, forms and symbols, books and mythology – are all for the purification of the soul, for the burning away of dross so that the spirit can shine clear. Many souls and many civilizations need these things, and the pouring of beauty, art, colour, words, on the altar of God, is a crying need for some souls, and its fulfilment has enriched the world, and produced great saints, just as it has also produced fanaticism and even war.

Progressing towards the ripe or supreme stage of Bhakti, it is vital for us to remember that the ultimate Brahman of the jnanis is also the God of Love of the bhaktas; it is Brahman seen in the relative aspect, seen 'through the mist of the senses'. Vivekananda used the metaphor of clay, from which many things can be made and these things are identical in substance, but as long as they all made in forms, the forms are separate. Ishwara – personal God – is the highest possible reading of the Absolute by the human mind. Creation is eternal; so is Ishwara. Ishwara is as real as the Universe.

Bhakti floats smoothly with the current of our human nature; it does not cut sharply across it as Jnana is bound to do. Development is slower, but flowers more naturally; it is our nature to love, to stand in a relationship with someone. The personal God is an aspect of the Ultimate; we never forget the clay of which all is made. Similarly the great Incarnation might be thought of as a bas-relief carved on the wall of a cave; he has his form and name, but we never forget that he is a part – a substance, a projection – of the Absolute; when we see him, we think of the wall of the cave also. All the metaphors – including Ramakrishna's metaphor of the Absolute as water, boundless and beyond sight and comprehension, but taking form and shape in an Incarnation as a piece of ice under the cooling influence of the bhakta's love (whether or not the sun of Knowledge (Jnana) eventually melts it again) – all show that the ultimate point reach by the bhakti and the jnani, is the same.

In Vivekananda's words :

When next you hear a man delivering a great intellectual lecture against the worship of the Incarnations of God, get hold of him and ask him what *his* idea of God is, what *he* understands by 'omnipotence', 'omnipresence' and all similar terms, beyond the spelling of the words. He really means nothing by them; he cannot formulate as their meaning any idea unaffected by his own human nature; he is no better off in this matter than the man in the street who has not read a single book . . . Religion is, after all, realization [experience] and we must make the sharpest distinction between talk and intuitive experience. What we experience in the depth of our souls is realization. Nothing indeed is so uncommon as common sense in regard to this matter.

The devotion and love the bhakta gives to Ishwara, to a personal God, is made more natural still by his love of an Incarnation, however he regards him or by whatever name he calls him. So from time to time, Ishwara manifests all of Himself that one human vessel can hold, in an Incarnation of God, and spirituality, which was drying up in the world, breaks out once more. The saints, the prophets, the Incarnations; still they come. In Hinduism, many Incarnations are recognized. As Ramakrishna said, 'When an Incarnation comes, a tidal wave of spirituality breaks upon the world, and people feel spirituality almost full in the air.' Vivekananda pointed out that every soul is destined to achieve perfection, in the end, after many lives; and future lives will be shaped by our thoughts and actions in this one. For this, the shaping of our own destinies, outside help is sometimes needed. Books may help at a certain stage, but to quicken the spirit the impulse must come from another soul, the guru. We will consider later, in the teachings on meditation, the qualifications required in a great guru; they are very high indeed, and many were the warnings Ramakrishna gave against the dangers of a false guru; better no guru at all, except the mind of the student, until the true great guru comes, as he will, at the right time. When the ground has been prepared, the seed is sown; so a certain fitness in the student is necessary also.

Temporary religious excitement that does not last is of little use. It may be a beginning, but only a beginning. Deceit, insincerity, lack of tolerance, totally immoral living, egotism – none of these things is likely to put out a spiritual call which will be heard and answered – except possibly by a guru equally unworthy. Purity, in the chemical sense of something undiluted, straight from source – a real longing and thirst after religious knowledge – and strong perseverance which is prepared to fight on for a lifetime, many lifetimes, if necessary – these are the ingredients.

'When the power that attracts the light of religion in the receiving soul is full and strong,' said Vivekananda, 'the power which answers to that attraction and sends in light, does come, as a matter of course.' It is the same truth here as in all Rama-krishna's teachings on every aspect of religion; the natural in-evitability, preceded always by striving and effort on our part. 'The wind of God's grace is always blowing – *but* you must first unfurl your sail to catch the wind.' And if we do not feel that we can unfurl very much – if we are only half-ready? 'Then make a beginning,' says Ramakrishna, 'and *pray*. Pray for more strength, more love, more longing – whatever is needed.' Always we come back to the same Vendantic point : we must make the effort, but our own ego, our own will, our own personality – these things do not stand alone, the great Blessedness is there, ready to answer and flood in; whether to bhakta or jnani, it is the same Blessedness.

In Indian philosophy, the 'germ of spiritual wisdom' con-veyed to the disciple by the guru, is the mantra. Most world religions have their own prayer or holy word, and those people who belong to no specific religion or orthodoxy, often evolve, almost instinctively, a word, a prayer of their own which is especially holy and blessed to them. We will consider this in more detail when we come to consider meditation, but from the point of view of philosophy, Vivekananda taught that the whole of this universe has both name and form. Form is the outer crust, the name or idea is the inner essence or kernel. In the universe, Brahman first manifested as name and then as form – that is, the universe. As with 'Logos' or 'word', and as we find in St John's Gospel : 'In the Beginning was the word, and the word was with God, and the word *was* God.'

The ultimate mantra which is said to contain all other mantras within itself, is 'Om', made in fact by the letters 'AUM', com-prising all possible sounds : 'A' is the first sound as the lips open, and 'M' the bringing together again of the lips. Since it is a sound, a symbol, and not a word in some language with a specific mean-ing, it can be used by all nations and all people whatever their language or religion.

The mantra is not used as some kind of magic, but it becomes a thought of great power, used not only in meditation but running continually through the mind in the day, in the bus queue, when walking, when doing housework; instead of vague day dreaming, or worry, or harmful thinking, the continuous sound of the mantra – whatever it may be – sounding within the mind, brings the same natural, relaxed but alert joy which the lover feels when thinking of the beloved, or the child when it cries 'Mother', instinctively; or as those who love the sound of the sea like to hear its continuing movement sounding in the background, or the murmur of wood pigeons causes some people to relax as soon as they hear it. (Pigeons cooing also irritate some people and cause them to become tense; just as the drone of pop music from a transistor radio can soothe some people sitting on a beach or in a dentist's chair, while it drives others to a fury which causes immediate tension.)

Sound is important; what matters is the association of the sound, the feeling it arouses, and our reaction to it. The mantra, especially when given by the guru, comes to us with all the right associations, and it is full of peace, joy and holiness because it is used in meditation. It has been said that if we walk along with the mantra sounding in our minds, we walk bathed in light and surrounded by God. In some form or other, the repetition of a special word or prayer, by those of all religions or none, has been used and valued from primitive times, and by all races.

Before Vivekananda went on to describe the supreme devotion, 'ripe Bhakti', which had passed the early stages, it is noticeable that as well as the means of attainment which might be expected : purity, control of the senses, self-restraint, continuing thought of God, truthfulness, sincerity, doing good to others without gain to oneself, Ahimsa (not injuring others by thought, word, or deed – harmlessness in a positive rather than a passive sense) great strength of character, and the toughening of the body to acquire physical strength, and the toughening of the mind so that we become mentally strong – to all these he added one other vital ingredient which sometimes surprised Victorian orthodox Westerners.

The important ingredient was 'cheerfulness'. He even said on one occasion that if one absolutely *insisted* on being depressed, one had better stay at home and not infect others with the poison. One enquirer who had been accustomed to long-faced solemnity in the religious, asked him if he ever stopped laughing. 'Only when I have the stomach ache,' replied this man of the greatest seriousness and earnestness. To him, cheerfulness and laughter were of the essence of joy; but he detested and warned very seriously against a false heartiness, or an excessive frivolity which, he said, 'is quite as objectionable as too much sad seriousness, and all religious realization is possible only when the mind is in a steady, peaceful condition of harmonious equilibrium. It is thus that one may begin to learn how to love the Lord.'

A disciple said of Ramakrishna, 'Whether grave or playful, always an atmosphere of blissfulness enveloped him and radiated from him. He declared frequently that he would have nothing to do with a religion that had not a laugh in it.' Ramakrishna, however, also rebuked gently or withdrew from, those who were excessively frivolous or hilarious in the wrong way. 'Harmonious equilibrium' brings us back again to the harmony that expresses itself in laughter, and the steadiness that is also needed; without both, we are back again in chaos.

Now, as we pass to Para-Bhakti, or Supreme Devotion, for which all things so far, including rituals, forms, mantra, are purifiers, we have to consider the greatest purifier of all, and it is exactly the same as the ultimate purifier in Jnana, and in all the yogas: renunciation.

The renunciation of the jnani is the toughest; he has to tear himself away from all bondage to nature right from the beginning and stand alone. Of all renunciation that of the bhakta is the most natural, most easy-flowing. It is the same as we see around us all in forms of love. A man loves a woman; he outgrows this love, loves another, and marries her; the first love simply drops away. He has gone past it. A woman loves a doll when she is a child; when she has her own baby, she does not need to renounce the doll; it is outgrown. A man passionately loves his own city; this may grow into a love for his own country, and the city becomes less important. Then he loves the whole world. A man loves the pleasures of the senses until he discovers that he has a mind; then, unlike the animal who lives only in the senses, he finds a higher pleasure; and in time, a higher joy still in the spirit, higher than in senses or intellect. The bhakta does not suppress or cut off any of his emotions. On the contrary, he intensifies them and directs them to God.

The bhakta sees little use in talking of detachment unless he is at the same time becoming attached to something more lovable, more worth a lifetime's devotion. And gradually he comes to see that everything he loves and everybody he loves is an expression of God, the Lord – of what the jnani calls 'That'. 'He shining, everything shines. It is through His light that all things shine.'

Even in the lowest form of attraction there is a spark of that bliss which is 'the Lord Himself' and in all human relationships – when husband kisses wife, when mother fondles baby, friend rushes to friend – the Lord is there. It is not the lump of flesh, the arrangement of cells in a body, which we love. In the famous words which sum this up : 'None, O beloved, ever loved the husband for the husband's sake; it is the Atman, the Lord who is within, for whose sake the husband is loved.' So with the love of husband and wife, parent and child, and all loving relationships. When the bhakta comes to see this great truth, and not only to see it but to experience it, then more and more he finds that 'in all faces shines to him the Face of Faces' until at last he reaches an outlook where only he and the Lord exist, he plays a part on a stage in which he and his God are the only two actors; he wakes each morning knowing that every face he sees, even the angry face of a would-be enemy, is the face of the Lord; like the monk who, bitten by a snake, said, 'A messenger came to me from the beloved', and he who was beaten by a bully and then revived by milk given by his fellow-monks, said, 'He who just now beat me, is now giving me milk.'

The ultimate aim – and it is a very high one, and not achieved overnight – is a universal love in which love is given for love's sake only. In the lowest form of human love, for instance, one loves for one's own pleasure; in a higher form, there is mutual love on both sides; the highest love is totally unselfish, asks nothing, and seeks only to love. By the very law of love, it *will* receive love in return; but the motive is not begging, it is giving and loving. Vivekananda says :

Object after object is taken up, and the inner ideal is successively projected on them all; and all such external objects are found inadequate as exponents of the ever-expanding inner ideal, and are naturally rejected one after another. At last the aspirant begins to think that it is vain to try to realize the ideal in external objects, that all external objects are as nothing compared with the ideal itself.

The bhakta does not neglect his wife; she too is a manifestation. He sees God *in* her, but he does not stop there and make an idol of her; his love is for its own sake, it is love given freely to every stick and stone in the universe, some loved closely and some at greater distance; some people are loved in constant, close daily love and service, some perhaps never even encountered. Ramakrishna advised the woman who could not meditate because her thoughts ran away to her baby nephew whom she was bringing up, to regard the child as the baby Krishna and serve him with the loving care of one who serves her God (which did not include spoiling and pampering him, for that would harm his spiritual progress, and who wants to harm God?).

Equally, the love of God itself may be expressed by a special relationship which comes naturally to the devotee. To some natures a human relationship is always necessary. Jesus loved God as Father; millions, in consequence, have lived and died with the words 'Our Father' on their lips.

For those natures who are helped by thinking of God in a continual personal relationship, as Ramakrishna, who experienced realization of God through them all, particularly centred on God as 'Mother', one of the 'bhavas', or human representations of the Divine, becomes a part of living and thinking. The lowest form of this expression is Shanta; peaceful, quiet, gentle; it has not the greatest fire of love, but it is a beginning. Next is Dasya, the attitude of servant to Master; this relationship of loving and trusted servant to loving and ever-present Lord was often recommended by Ramakrishna. Next is Sakhya – friendship; this is coming closer to equality; there can be no awe between friends, no fear; complete frankness and openness; 'equal love flows in and out between the worshipper and his friendly God' said Vivekanada.

The innermost secrets of our hearts we may place before him with the great assurance of safety and support. God is viewed here as our playmate. We may well say that we are all playing in this universe. . . . If you are poor, enjoy that as fun, if you are rich, enjoy the fun of being rich, if dangers come, it is also good fun; if happiness comes, there is more good fun. God is our eternal playmate. How beautifully He is playing! . . . It is only when you forget that it is all play, and that you are also helping in the play, it is only then that misery and sorrow come; then the heart becomes heavy, then the world weighs upon you with tremendous power; but as soon as you give up the serious idea of reality as the characteristic of the changing incidents of this three minutes of life, and know it to be but a stage on which we are playing, helping Him to play, at once misery ceases for you. He plays in every atom; He is playing when He is building up earths, and suns and moons; He is playing with the human heart, with animals and plants, and oh bliss! we are His playmates!

It is noticeable that each of these bhavas – to which a lifetime is devoted – is approaching nearer and nearer to intimacy and is breaking down awe, for as long as there is awe, there is always a slight tinge of fear and a certain sense of separation.

The next, Vatsalya, is the love of God as our child; as the Christian at Christmas thinks of the baby Jesus. This avoids the fear-creating sense of a God of Power; parents do not feel afraid of their own child. One does not *ask* the child for anything; one gives; and a parent will sacrifice his comfort and his own life for the child.

The highest human representation of love is known as Madhura – sweet – and is the love of lover for lover, or wife for husband. It is found in Christianity in the nun who regards herself as the bride of Christ. But to those still involved in worldly duties, particularly to those with sex-experience, this approach sometimes has its dangers, as has been found in some of the Hindu cults. Taken in its purest form, however, as was originally intended, it is the ultimate 'madness of love' in which nothing matters but the beloved, where there is no desire whatever for anything that exists, except the beloved; when union with the beloved is the whole goal of life.

To those who came to him, Ramakrishna often recommended the attitude of servant to beloved Master, of loving friend to friend, or of child to parent; but each nature is different, and it is here that the great guru, watching the seed grow, sees in which form it will flower. Like all approaches, none of these is obligatory, but many souls have reached incredible heights through one of these approaches; and the strengthening power and security of one such loving approach, sustained through a lifetime, has been experienced again and again in those who have the bhakta-nature.

Whatever the approach or the relationship, one word is much beloved in the highest stages of Bhakti, and inevitably so. It is the word 'Apratikulya'. This means, a deep conviction that nothing that happens, or can happen, is against us. All things – struggles, difficulties, pain, death itself – cannot frustrate the bhakta, they all came from Him, therefore they are all a blessing, a part of the play, something to be used; a burning-away of the dross of our ego. The contented acceptance of the bhakta does not imply a lazy fatalism; it implies, in Vivekananda's words:

a state of the mind in which it has no interests, and naturally knows nothing that is opposed to it. In this state of sublime resignation everything in the way of attachment goes away completely, except that one all-absorbing love to Him in whom all things live and move and have their being. This attachment of love to God is indeed one that does not bind the soul but effectively breaks all its bondages.

So here, too, the bhakta, like the jnani, is moving towards a consciousness which is universal. Vivekananda sums it up for us : 'He finds Him in the saint's saintliness as well as in the wicked man's wickedness; because he has Him already seated in glory in his own heart, as the one Almighty, inextinguishable Light of Love, which is ever shining and eternally present.'

In his final words on the subject, he brings us to the heights to which the jnani travels :

We all begin with love for ourselves, and the unfair claims of the little self make even love selfish; at last, however, comes the full blaze of light in which this little self is seen to have become one with the infinite. Man himself is transfigured in the presence of this Light of Love, and he realizes at last the beautiful and inspiring truth that Love, the Lover, and the Beloved are one.

7

KARMA YOGA: THE YOGA OF DEDICATED WORK

The word 'karma' is derived from the Sanskrit 'Kri', 'to do'. All action is karma. When linked with a belief in reincarnation, then technically karma also implies the results of our past actions, possibly in past lives. But in Karma Yoga the word is taken to imply work. Psychologically, any work, any action, any thought that produces an effect is called a karma; as Ramakrishna said, every moment that we live, we are working; in breathing our lungs are working, even meditation is a form of work. When asked what *kind* of work should be undertaken, he replied that it is not that one kind of work is right, and another wrong; what matters is that work, too, must be used to create detachment, purity, the burning-away of the dross, so that the 'great lion' which is within each one of us may be more clearly manifested.

If we watch two men working at, perhaps, a great humanitarian work, one will be fully aware that in serving humanity he is privileged, he is, as it were, a tool; if he dropped dead, another would take his place; he is blessed that he is able to do the work. So he works like a master, not a slave, with joy and detachment. Even if the choice was not his in the first place, he does the work selflessly; he does not feel that he *owns* it, the sense of ego is not there. The next man, engaged on exactly the same work, may be attached to it, furious if it goes wrong, angry if his name is not trumpeted as a benefactor; as Ramakrishna often warned, the great danger of Karma Yoga and indeed of all work, is that however noble the intention at the beginning, somewhere along the way egotism and attachment tend to creep in. Some mothers may, as they say, 'love their children to death' – 'smother-love', not mother-love. Such a mother works and slaves for the child; but she either alienates, spoils, or enslaves the child. Another mother is 'firm' and 'detached' – which could again be a covering for egotism, and might mean that the child grows up starved of warm demonstrative affection. The rich man with many servants sometimes makes himself a slave to 'duty' – he binds himself and his children in an endless round of social engagements in 'living as our station in life requires' – he is a self-created slave and not really the master of his work, or of his own life.

As with all the yogas, what matters is the mind and its attitude; not only what is done, but *why* it is done. Even if we must do work which we did not choose, but which must be done never the less, then what matters is our attitude towards it. It is amazing how deeply we become involved and attached, and the illusion of 'it all depends on me', which in theory ought to make us more conscientious, in fact wears down our nerves and creates egotism. Nothing depends on us. It is our privilege, as Vivekananda often pointed out, to work; the bhakta serves his God in all, the karma Yogi may do the same, or if he has no religious belief he may simply work and serve, out of love and self-abnegation, compassion and the joy of activity; he too is burning away dross. In the words of Vivekananda :

It is sheer nonsense on the part of any man to think that he is born to help the world; it is simply pride, it is selfishness insinuating itself in the form of virtue . . . when you give something to a man and expect nothing – do not even expect the man to be grateful – his ingratitude will not tell upon you, because you never expected anything, never thought you had any right to anything in the way of a return. You gave him what he deserved; his own Karma got it for him; your Karma made you the carrier thereof. Why should you be proud of having given away something? You are the porter that carried the money or other kind of gift, and the world deserved it by its own Karma.

This degree of humility and detachment – in even the most difficult or boring work, performed with the joy of the artist who paints because he takes joy in it, and is glad of the chance – is not easy to achieve. In the West, as Vivekananda often said in praise, hard work and efficiency and self-discipline are admirable virtues which he could see that the East frequently lacked; but egotism crept in only too often, and the nervous tension which reacts in the form of worry, guilt, and nervous exhaustion; slavery, in fact. Heart disease, high blood pressure, ulcers, nervous break-downs – early death may kill the affluent Westerner, just as gruelling hours of work on too little food in bad conditions can cause early death in the East. Anxiety might almost be called the Western disease. Again, in the words of Vivekananda :

It is a very hard thing to understand, but you will come to learn in time that nothing in the universe has power over you until you allow it to exercise such a power. Nothing has power over the Self of man, until the Self becomes a fool and loses independence. So by non-attachment you overcome and deny the power of anything to act upon you. It is very easy to say that nothing has the right to act upon you until you allow it to do so; but what is the true sign of the man who really does not allow anything to work upon him, who is neither happy nor unhappy when acted upon by the external world? The sign is that good or ill fortune causes no change in his mind; in all conditions he continues to remain the same.

The karma Yogi expects difficulties, and he will certainly encounter them. But if he believes in God, he will work for God; if he seeks to serve others and has no religious belief in the conventional sense, he will work for the joy of serving; he will work for the work's sake; and if his work benefits anybody – and all work does, in some way, even if we scrub a floor or write a letter – he will not regard himself as a benefactor. He was doing what it was his nature to do; careful work.

Edward Carpenter, that great Englishman (who once visited a jnani in the East for instruction, and several times visited and spoke to Vivekananda), spoke very little of his own religious beliefs. He was often referred to as 'a social reformer', which considerably annoyed him; in his seventies, when he was a deeply loved and respected figure who had spent a lifetime doing good to an infinite number of people and noble causes, he said :

I have sometimes been accused of taking to a rather plain and Bohemian way of life, of associating with manual workers, of speaking at street corners, growing fruit, making sandals, writing, or whatnot, at great cost to my own comfort, and with ulterior and artificial purpose – as of reforming the world. But I can safely say, that in any such case I have done the thing primarily and simply because of the joy I had in doing it, and to please myself. If the world or any part of it should in consequence insist on being reformed, that is not my fault. . . . Perhaps people should endeavour, more than they do, to express or liberate their own real and deep-rooted needs and feelings. Then in doing so they will probably liberate the expression of the lives of thousands of others, and so will have the pleasure of helping, without the unpleasant sense of laying anyone under an obligation.

There speaks the karma Yogi. It may be suggested that the words 'to please myself' suggest egotism; but Carpenter was of course referring to his great Self, or Atman; his ego-self would probably have preferred to stay at home and to have lazed comfortably in the usual life-style of the well-to-do Victorian gentleman.

But again, it may be objected, he could choose what he did. What of the millions who must find what work they can? But the way they work and their attitude towards it still lies in their own hands. A house-painter might not ideally *choose* to spend his time standing on a ladder in an east wind painting the guttering of your house; but that is his work; and one man will rush through it and make a poor job of it, thinking only of the money he will earn; and another may go over it with endless care – 'Because I could not look myself in the face if I left a badly painted drainpipe in *that* condition. I like to do a good job,' he says.

The concept of working like a master, not a slave, may imply that we can be as slovenly as we like; but to anyone with the nature of the karma Yogi (even if he has never heard the word) that would be like telling a devoted parent, whose life is dedicated to his children, that he is free to neglect or ill-treat them if he wishes. He does *not* wish!

Work is a part of life; we must come to terms with it; we must use it, or it will use us. To turn again to the words of Vivekananda :

This world's wheel within wheel is a terrible mechanism; if we put our hands in it, as soon as we are caught, we are gone. We all think that when we have done a certain duty, we shall be at rest; but before we have done a part of that duty, another is already in waiting. We are all being dragged along by this mighty complex worldmachine. There are only two ways out of it; one is to give up all concern with the machine, to let it go and stand aside, to give up our desires; the way of Jnana Yoga. That is very easy to say, but is almost impossible to do. I do not know whether in twenty millions of men, one can do that. The other way is to plunge into the world and learn the secret of work, and that is the way of Karma Yoga. Do not fly away from the wheels of the world-machine, but stand inside it and learn the secret of work. Through this machinery itself, is the way out.

The way out, as in all the yogas, lies always in self-abnegation, in renunciation of the ego; of a continual purifying – and in joy. The 'master' of work, works through love. The man who says he has no religion but who works joyfully and selflessly, and he who willingly works for others, is moving further and further away

E

from his own small self. The great teaching of the Gita is that we have the right to work, but not to the fruits of work. This does not mean that we must not accept an honest day's pay for an honest day's work; it means that we perform devoted work, done as beautifully as possible, and (if we believe in God) given to God – it is His. In any case, he ultimately did the work, we are the tool in his hands, and lucky are we to be used. A great painter may give every moment, every thought, every breath, forgetting even to bother about meal times, to the creation of a masterpiece; for a time he has been 'outside himself' – his own wants were forgotten in the work; and then he may give the picture to a friend and never see it again. There is something in us all which instinctively respects devoted work, done in detachment and without desire for praise or thanks. There are many who cannot as yet find their way to religion, but their whole lives are given to service, whether direct service to humanity, or to their work; and the world is the richer because they exist, while they themselves are drawing nearer and nearer to that goal which they do not yet recognize.

'He denies the existence of that Light, standing there with the Light radiating from him,' was said of a selfless 'non-religious' worker for humanity. And, of the old woman in her small street, who made it her unpaid job to carry parcels of clothes for famine relief to the depot, because the people with cars 'were too busy', a neighbour said, 'She says she is too old for work – but she will work for others till she dies. And nobody will ever hear about it, or thank her.'

'Selfless dedicated work' is a phrase that suggests fame; the great philanthropist; the great humanitarian. The essence of all the yogas, on the contrary, as Vivekananda said, is 'unity in variety'. This, he said, is the plan of creation. 'However men and women may vary individually, there is unity in the background.'

We tend sometimes to judge others by our own ideals or our own capacities. 'All the men and women in any society are not of the same mind, capacity, or of the same power to do things; they must have different ideals, and we have no right to sneer at any ideal.'

In the Hindu system of morality, Vivekananda points out, from very ancient times, the work and duties of different people have been recognized, and the 'householder', not necessarily meaning one who owns a house, but what, in the West, we might call 'the laity' – (those who are not monks, those who have not renounced the world) – has different work and duties from the Sannyasin (the monk) and the student. The Hindu began life as a student, through childhood and youth; then he married and he became a householder; in old age he retired and became more detached from worldly affairs and duties, and lastly a total detachment brought him to the life almost of a Sannyasin, he and his wife living simply as spiritual companions. A lifetime's spiritual endeavour could then be garnered, while they both contentedly prepared for the approach of death; so that old age became the quiet crown of life, not something to be dreaded. These stages were in later time reduced to two – either householder or monk – but the general attitude towards both was the same as before. The monk is free to go straight to the goal, the householder comes to it gradually through performance of his duties while at the same time he continues his spiritual progress; Ramakrishna had much to say about this difficult balancing feat, as we shall see later.

The life of the married man, says Vivekananda, in speaking of Karma Yoga, is as great as that of the celibate who has devoted himself to religious work. Also, 'the scavenger in the street is quite as great and glorious as the king on his throne. Take him off his throne, make him do the work of the scavenger, and see how he fares. Take up the scavenger and see how he will rule.' The first beginnings of the caste system had this idea of the trade-guild in which each trade had its own way of life, its own self-respect; but as always in human affairs, over the years it became degraded and crystallized into contempt or hatred for what was regarded as low-caste; its cruelties appalled Vivekananda, but he saw that caste reform in India must be gradual, one cannot suddenly smash open the life-style of thousands of years. In the West we talk much of equality, but we have our own caste systems, less open; it has truly been said, with justifiable sarcasm, that in the West all men are equal, but some are more equal than others.

Great men are often remembered for actions or teachings which differed from what was expected. Ramakrishna is sometimes referred to as 'an ecumenical saint' because of his teachings about the oneness of all religions, though the description is inadequate and only touches one part of his life's experience and teachings; he is also described vaguely, on occasions, as someone who brought Bhakti into the foreground of religious thought again.

Today, some other aspect of the great harmony he was playing might have been especially noticed; we cannot tell. Those who really cared, rejoiced at the whole harmony, and still do. In the case of Vivekananda it was perhaps his teaching on Jnana which so lit up his Western audiences; his 'you are *That*', his emphasis on the greatness in man; and his emphasis on Karma Yoga, which surprised the energetic Westerners, who had previously associated Oriental philosophy, especially Hinduism and yoga, with passivity and non-action.

But the monumental difficulties of the work he undertook are sometimes forgotten. To establish what is today the largest monastery in India, with famine relief work, education and hospitals on a gargantuan scale, balanced with the teaching on meditation and the co-operation of all those devotees who are still 'in the world' and not monastic; to bring Vedanta to the countries of the world – we can see the results of this now, but he started, in his lifetime, with a handful of young men who had been Rama-krishna's disciples, staying in a rented rat-infested house. The scale of the suffering in India, and the longing for meditation and inner peace in the West, was so enormous that it might have daunted even a millionaire with a ready-made organization, and he had no money whatever and did not wish for organizations, beyond the barest minimum necessary.

In India the service of the poor was not accepted as readily as being a suitable life for monastics as it was in the West. For Brahmin boys to heal – and therefore to touch – lepers, or indeed to eat and drink with Westerners who were regarded as 'unclean' – this meant the breaking down of taboos which inevitably resulted in hostility at first. Nothing happened smoothly. Watching him through the eyes of close disciples and friends, and reading his own letters which show the perpetual strain on his nervous system and failing health as he moved about the world, we can see that in practising Karma Yoga he struggled and suffered as we all do. He never wrote to disciples or friends as one speaking from serene heights, but as one fellow-warrior to another, in the midst of difficulties.

His English disciple, Margaret Noble (Sister Nivedita), wrote of him :

I found in his own country another point of view, from which he was very, very human. And here, though the results of his efforts may have been choicer, or more enduring, than those of most of us, yet they were wrought at the self-same cost of having to toil on in darkness and uncertainty and only now and then emerging into light.

The mixture of 'acceptance of what happens' and the continuous demands of great projects which he could never live to see fully developed often tore at him.

In those last five and a half years particularly which were his crowning gift to his own people, he stood for work without attachment, or work for impersonal ends, as one of the highest expressions of the religious life. . . . But in India, the head and front of the demand made on a monastic order is that it produces saints. And the value of the monk who, instead of devoting himself to maintaining the great tradition of the super-conscious life, turns back to help society upwards, has not in the past been clearly understood. . . . Men would be sent out from the Monastery to give relief in famine-stricken areas, to direct the sanitation of a town, or to nurse the sick and dying in a pilgrim-centre. One man started an orphanage and industrial school. . . . Another established a teaching nucleus in the South. These were, said the Swami, the 'sappers and miners' of the army of religion. His schemes, however, went much further.

He was consumed with a desire for the education of Indian women and for the scientific and technical education of the country. How the impersonal motive multiplies the power to suffer, only those who have seen can judge.

She saw that it was inevitable that the Hindu ideal of the religious life as being one of total detachment from worldly matters was, as she wrote, 'so clear and so deeply established that only at great cost to himself could a man carry it into a fresh channel. Has anyone realized the pain endured by the sculptor of a new ideal?'

And yet in the West to regard humanitarian work, vital as it was, as *second* in importance to giving 'spiritual food' – for when a man is fed, he may still be unhappy and unfulfilled – to regard the discovery of the Self within, in meditation, as the highest goal of all; to preach Jnana and Bhakti as *well* as purely humanitarian aims, and to avoid dogma, this, also, brought difficulties from the other extreme – and more 'pain endured'.

'It took the form of a play upon two different ideals, of which either was highest in its own world, and yet each, to those who believed in its fellow, almost a crime,' said this disciple.

Vivekananda's creation of a harmony did not always happen harmoniously for *him*. One of the greatest benefits that has come to us from that disciple – quite apart from her work for India – is her book about her own observations, experience, and discussions with Vivekananda, *The Master As I Saw Him*, and her collecting-in of his letters to friends, disciples, and, indeed, to people without number all over the world. To read these published letters, side by side with the published discourses, lectures and talks he gave, takes us into the mind of one who was not only a mighty worker of almost incredible energy, but sometimes 'a lion caught in a net', a man exhausted, ill, battered by life's waves and facing discouragement and anxiety like the rest of us. This completely removes any impression that he sat nobly on Olympic heights, telling humanity what it should do. He lived life out, and everything he taught, he himself practised under conditions of appalling difficulty. Side by side with this, again, we can set the comments of those who met him or who spent even a short time with him; and the word 'bliss' which they use about him, has a much stronger ring of truth when it is taken in conjunction with his personal letters which show at what cost that bliss was maintained. It is the spirituality shining *through* the human difficulties – plus the sense of humour which never seems to have left him, and the continual love, which make his teachings on Karma Yoga ring so truly in the ears of those also struggling in the grip of life. It may be said that, like some great mountain climbers, he came into the world better equipped than most of us (spiritually speaking) to climb life's highest peaks; he could cope with a spiritual Everest; we, perhaps, could not. But this fact illustrates a part of the whole Vedantic teaching; each one of us brings into the world the equipment he needs, and is going to use; Vivekananda may have been marvellously equipped, but he had higher mountains – and more of them – than most of us will have to face. His extreme gentleness with those he found struggling with burdens which might not have worried *him*, but which were almost more than their 'spiritual equipment' could carry, can be compared with his blast of energy, strength – or even anger – where it was needed by the spiritually well-equipped, from whom more could be expected. He spoke always to the lion within each one, and an American disciple wrote of him that this had a tonic effect; something long dormant was awakened, and instinctively responded. He was sometimes accused in India of emphasizing Karma Yoga – especially in its aspect of humanitarian work – too much.

Equally, in the West, the importance he placed on meditation, renunciation and, for those who were ready for it, celibacy, was often queried. But he strode on doggedly, for he had set himself the task of creating a harmony, and while he said that it is indeed possible for some natures to devote themselves entirely and exclusively to *one* of the yogas, and reach ultimate Realization through that one path alone, for most people, especially those living 'out in the world', a harmony of yogas, with one of the yogas prevailing most strongly, is most likely to create a life that is whole, integrated, and at peace with itself; then strength will grow.

One remark of Ramakrishna's had made a deep impression on him. Ramakrishna valued compassion very highly; but he said that the compassion itself came from God, and in serving others we do in fact serve God; and this fitted beautifully with the ideal, also, of the Jnana Yogi, who serves the Self in others. This removes any tinge of the condescension or self-praise that sometimes stains compassion, and it revolutionized Vivekananda's thinking, as he himself said :

Let us do good because it is good to do good; he who does good work even to get to heaven, binds himself down, says the Karma Yogi. Any work that is done with the least selfish motive, instead of making us free, forges one more chain for our feet. So the only way, is to give up all the fruits of work, to be unattached to them. Know that this world is not we, nor are we this world; that we are really not the body; that we really do not work. We are the Self, eternally at rest and at peace. Why should we be bound by anything?

As always, we come back to the same point so often made by Ramakrishna : 'Bondage is of the mind, freedom is of the mind.'

It all lies in our own attitude of mind towards what we do. The monk's duty may mean a total renunciation; a married man must earn money to support his family. We all have different work to do. In the words of Ramakrishna :

A householder, of course, needs money, for he has a wife and children. He should save up to feed them. They say that the bird and the sannyasi, [the monk] should not provide for the future. But the mother bird brings food in her mouth for her chicks; so she too provides. A householder needs money. He has to support his family.

If a householder is a genuine devotee, he performs his duties without attachment; he surrenders the fruit of his work to God – his gain or loss, his pleasure or pain – and day and night he prays for devotion and for nothing else. This is called motiveless work, the performance of duty without attachment. A sannyasi, too, must do all his work in that spirit of detachment; but he has no worldly duties to attend to, like a householder.

Ramakrishna taught always that in serving others one is really serving God who dwells in all beings, and so one is in fact purifying oneself through this selfless work. But the danger of complacency – of developing a mood of secret self-congratulation on one's own nobility of service – is always checked by the remembrance that it is our *privilege* to work, and to serve in a spirit of detachment – to serve God, as Ramakrishna said, 'not through men alone but through animals and other living beings as well'. But we cannot congratulate ourselves that we are *helping* the universe; and this thought will keep us humble. It is God alone who creates, preserves, acts and helps; at our best we are His instruments. In one of his best-known and often-quoted teachings, Ramakrishna says :

Helping others, doing good to others – this is the work of God alone, who for men has created the sun and moon, father and mother, fruits, flowers and corn. The love that you see in parents is God's love : He has given it to them to preserve His creation. The compassion that you see in the kind-hearted, is God's compassion : He has given it to them to protect the helpless.

But what if a man or woman becomes perfectly selfless through work, service and self-sacrifice for others, but does not yet believe in the ultimate Brahman, the Self, or in a personal God ? What of the agnostic or the honest atheist who does not query the belief of others, but cannot accept it himself ?

The yogas all lead to one point, which must be achieved before final Realization can be experienced; and that point is a total renunciation of the small self, the ego : self-abnegation. And Vivekananda answers the question for us :

Although a man has not studied a single system of philosophy, although he does not believe in any God and never has believed, although he has not prayed even once in his whole life, if the simple power of good actions has brought him to that state where he is ready to give up his life and all else for others, he has arrived at the same point to which the religious man will come through his prayers and the philosopher through his knowledge; and so you may find that the philosopher, the worker, and the devotee all meet at one point, that one point being self-abnegation. . . . So Karma, Bhakti and Jnana all meet here.

In the end, all work, all activity, may drop away; the need for it has passed. But, in the homely words of Ramakrishna, *first*, work must be done.

God is now doing all these works through you. When they are finished, you will not return to them. The housewife finishes her household duties, feeds everyone, including the menservants and maidservants, and then goes to take her bath. She doesn't come back then, even if people shout for her.

And that point is reached, the point where the soul goes forward, in all the yogas, when the small self has been conquered, when self-abnegation has burned away everything that stands in the way, however long the path, however many falls on the way; and that applies to the Karma Yogi, even if he does not regard himself as a religious man: 'Karma, Bhakti and Jnana all meet here'.

Workers in all religions won Vivekananda's deep respect. He had a particular love and reverence for Buddha, who is often regarded as a great jnani and is revered for his meditation. Vivekananda regraded him as a jnani-worker, acting absolutely without personal motives, ready to lay down his own life to save even an animal, and making no claims for himself. He worshipped Buddha as a perfect combination of heart, brain and soul-power, working compassionately for others without tiring; a giant among the world's spiritual teachers.

But the obscure and unknown whom he met in his travels in India and the West often won his admiration and he said he gained great blessing by even meeting them; from them, too, he learned. He found devoted and selfless workers in many places. In the course of his early wanderings in India he was once besieged by crowds asking for instruction, and for three days he taught them and it did not occur to anyone that he might need food. When at last they went away, a very poor and low-caste man told him that he was worried to see him without food or drink for so long, and though caste taboos forbade him to offer food to a monk, and he risked punishment or banishment, yet though he was afraid of what might happen to him, he cooked food and gave it to Vivekananda, who said later:

Out of the kindness of his heart, even though he feared the consequences, he brought me the cooked food. I doubted at that time whether it would have been more palatable if Indra, the King of the Devas should have held a cup of nectar in a golden basin before me. I shed tears of love and gratitude, and I thought, 'Thousands of such large-hearted men live in lowly huts, and we despise them as low castes and untouchables!' When I became well-acquainted with the Maharaja, I told him of the noble act of this man. Accordingly, within a few days the latter was called to the presence of the Prince. Frightened, beyond words, the man came, shaking all over, thinking that some dire punishment was to be inflicted upon him. But the Maharaja praised him and put him beyond all want.

In the last year of his life, Vivekananda, who knew he was a dying man and had handed over all responsibility for the monastery and for humanitarian work to others, was slowly moving away from life's involvements, making himself ready for departure. But sometimes he said, 'Oh, it is the *work* which still has power to entangle me!' He impressed again and again on the young novices the need for service. He was especially fond of some Santal labourers who worked in the monastery grounds. They were of low caste and had never eaten good food; Vivekananda served a small feast for them, which strictly speaking was against caste-rules, but they ate the food and said they had never eaten such good food before.

Their poverty, hard work and simplicity touched Vivekananda's heart. He said to the monks and novices of the monastery:

See how simple-hearted these poor illiterate people are! Can you mitigate their misery a little? . . . Sometimes I think within myself, 'What is the good of building monasteries and so forth! Why not sell them and distribute the money among the poor. What should we care for homes, we who have made the tree our shelter?

How can we have the heart to put a morsel to our mouths, when our countrymen have not enough wherewith to feed or clothe themselves! . . .' How I wish to demolish the barriers of 'Don't-touchism' and go out and bring together one and all, calling out, 'Come all ye that are poor and destitute, fallen and down-trodden! We are one, in the name of Ramakrishna!' Unless they are raised, this mother-land of ours will never awake! What are we good for, if we cannot provide them with food and clothing! . . . I see as clear as daylight that the same Brahman, the same Shakti that is in me, is in them as well!

A lay disciple said to him that it was altogether too much to hope that a harmony could be established in India amongst all the varying creeds, sects and religions, which could make them act in unison for a common purpose. This was certainly asking for the lion's roar, and it came.

Don't come here any more, if you think any task too difficult. Through the grace of the Lord, everything becomes easy of achievement. Your duty is to serve the poor and the distressed, without distinction of caste and creed. What business have you to think of the fruits of your action? Your duty is to go on working and everything will follow of itself. My method is to construct, and not to destroy that which is already existing. . . . You are all intelligent boys and profess to be my disciples – tell me what you have done. Can't you give away one life for the sake of others? . . . Let this body go in the service of others, and then I shall know that your coming to me has not been in vain.

In his final days, however, he reached the point Ramakrishna described when he referred to the housewife who after a long day's work is finished, goes off to bathe in the Ganges 'and you may call after her, but she will not return'.

The work was firmly established; he withdrew more and more into meditation. Ramakrishna was constantly in his mind. Even a reference to the rains (and possible famine) could not reach him; he simply replied that now he was making ready for death, though nobody saw then that he was speaking in terms of days, not years.

In his death he withdrew quietly and without fuss, passing away in meditation when death was not expected, when indeed his health had seemed a little better. Over and over in his last days he made the great point of Karma Yoga in his teaching, 'In serving all living beings one serves the Lord Himself', and he stressed the great lesson of selfless work; self-abnegation. He valued, too, the smallest, most hidden work done in ordinary daily duty; like his Master, he made no distinction in his service of people; the words 'great man' did not appeal to him. '*I* want to know how a great man speaks to his servants,' he said.

The Christian ethic of loving service, the Sermon on the Mount, and the parable of the good Samaritan, he revered; and he revered also the selfless work of those who had no religion or orthodoxy. Activity and work there will always be; what matters, as Ramakrishna said, is our attitude towards it. 'Bondage is of the mind; freedom is of the mind.' Even the smallest unselfish work leads us away from our own small ego; and every step away is a step in the right direction; service, said Ramakrishna and Vivekananda, is a privilege. And this is the meaning behind Karma Yoga.

8

RAJA YOGA: THE YOGA OF MEDITATION

I

The teachings of Ramakrishna and Vivekananda concerning meditation rest upon two vital principles. First, meditation is regarded as a means of discovering our true identity, and living in it fully. The answer to the question 'What am I?' is not going to be answered under the customary headings 'Name, sex, age, occupation' or even 'Personality, appearance, preferences, virtues and faults'. The meditator is going beyond all these, he will leave them behind, just as he will when he dies. He is seeking to find a Self which is eternal, and a joy and freedom which nothing can take from him. Secondly, meditation is not an act totally separate from the rest of life. Our daily life, rightly lived, illuminates our meditation, our meditation is the flame which keeps the lamp of daily living burning, as we express our true identity in the development of character. The young man who told Vivekananda that he could not control and calm his mind when he shut his eyes in meditation was told to open his eyes and find someone who needed help; his reply – that service of others might so weaken his health that he could not meditate – showed only too clearly that he was still identifying himself with his ego, his body, and a desire for comfort. On the other side of the same coin, Ramakrishna remarked that those who regarded philanthropy (organized by themselves, naturally) as the whole purpose of their existence would probably ask God Himself for hospitals and wells if He appeared before them; it would be better to ask Him for Himself, and then one might be trusted with philanthropy or indeed anything else.

Vivekananda, unlike his Master who was speaking mostly to Indians, had to explain to Western seekers that yoga means 'yoke', which is the conscious linking of the soul of man with the supreme Soul; that the Ultimate, the one Reality, is known as Brahman, which, manifested in man, is called the Atman. In his own words: 'The body is the external coating and the mind is the internal coating of the Atman, who is the real perceiver, the real enjoyer, the being in the body who is working the body by the means of the internal organ or the mind.' In his book on Raja Yoga, the yoga of meditation, he wrote : ' "I" covers a little consciousness and a vast amount of unconsciousness, while over it, and mostly unknown to it, is the super-conscious plane.'

But why has a wrong identification been made?

When the mind is studying the external object, it gets identified with it, and loses itself . . . the soul of man is like a piece of crystal, but it takes the colour of whatever is near it. That is the difficulty. That constitutes the bondage. We have taken the 'colour' of the body and have forgotten what we are. The crystal which reflects the colour red, thinks it is red. All our fears, all worries, anxieties, troubles, mistakes, weakness, evil, are from that great blunder, that we think we are bodies . . . the practice of meditation is pursued. The crystal knows what it is, takes its own colour.

He had to deal with the difference in usage of the word, in the West, where meditation so often means thinking about something, a sequence of thought.

If you take a long sentence, that is no meditation at all. Meditation means the mind is turned back upon itself. The mind stops all thought waves, and the world stops. You do not feel the body or anything else. That is the only way you ever get rest to your system. Not even the deepest sleep will ever give you such rest as that. The mind goes on jumping even in deepest sleep . . . you feel such pleasure in meditation, you become so light.

He always began with the one general principle :

Get hold of the mind. The mind is like a lake, and every stone that drops into it raises waves. The full moon is reflected in the water of the lake, but the surface is so disturbed that we do not see the reflection clearly. Let it be calm. The poor lake has got to throw the wave towards the stone whenever the stone is thrown in it. The mind must create the wave towards any sensation. Suppose we can withhold the mind. At once we are masters.

To become a Raja yogi in the full and specialized sense is not possible while living a life in the world, involved in duties. The Raja yogi must live far away from the bustle of life, deeply concentrated, able to withdraw into meditation, in a temperature that is equable and with food that is not too little or too much; he must live under the watchful eye of the guru. Meditation, for

those still involved in the world, is taken to imply a daily routine
– if possible, twice daily or more – while the rest of the day may
be a very active one. Even for this much meditation, Vivekananda
advised the care and instruction of a guru where this was possible.

Since such instruction is private and applicable only to the one
aspirant in each case, encouraging the nature of that one person
to develop in its own spiritual pattern, where a totally different
instruction might be given to another aspirant by the same guru,
obviously such private instruction, given by Ramakrishna,
Vivekananda, or any Swamis of the order, are not recorded. In
these two chapters the teachings on meditation are general, and
illustrations are given to show how varied may be the possible
types of meditation, and how definite the morality and ethics of
living upon which meditation must rest. All the teachings, state-
ments and advice given here are based on the words of Ramakrishna, Vivekananda, and the teachings of the Swamis of the
order, which today follow the same pattern and continue within
the same tradition. The teachings, being alive, may grow and
develop; meditation is not dead wood, it is a living tree. But the
deep root of the tree does not change.

Ramakrishna emphasized, 'The yogi is in control of his mind,
not the mind in control of the yogi', but he insisted, as did Vivekananda, that this was a long, patient work, and varied with the
nature of each person. But the broad basis of meditation rests,
in their teaching, on the eight steps of Pantanjali, and they are
as practical in life today, as in past centuries.

(1) *Yama.*   Non-injury, truthfulness, non-stealing, chastity
and the non-receiving of gifts. The last practice refers not to gifts
which are expressions of affection in a family or between friends,
but gifts which destroy the aspirant's independence of mind by
putting him under obligation to the giver.

(2) *Niyama.*   Cleanliness of body, purity of mind, contentment, austerity which must never go to the extreme of weakening
the body or mind, and devotion to God (in whatever aspect the
divine is worshipped). Contentment is taken to refer to acceptance of what cannot be changed in one's own life; it does not
imply absence of struggle, or aimless inertia; it is in particular
a warning against restlessness or envy. Vivekananda stressed also
that it does not mean contentment with other people's suffering;
I cannot say – using niyama as an excuse – that my neighbour's
suffering is probably doing him a great deal of spiritual good.

So it may be, but that is no business of mine. My job, ideally, is to serve him, or if this is not possible to send him thoughts of peace, strength and prayer.

The emphasis on chastity is not puritanical, but entirely practical. It is illustrated by the fact that not only yogis but the great saints and certainly the Incarnations of many religions have been celibate. Complete continence is necessary for the highest states of God-realization; as for the married, Ramakrishna taught his married disciples to move towards this ideal slowly, progressing through the early years of sex-life and raising a family, towards a growing detachment from the body and its desires, so that old age, far from being a stage of life to be dreaded, can be a time of peace when husband and wife can live together as spiritual companions, a time of detachment and joy when the daily meditation and spiritual progress of a lifetime can reach fruition. For those who wish to study the teachings on sex-energy, and the nerves of the spine and brain which are used in meditation, these are set out in full, there is nothing mysterious or esoteric about them; but, briefly, the energy of the nerve currents which are particularly used in sexual powers, are used in 'ojas' which, in meditation, travels up the spinal column; the 'sushumna' is the central channel of the spinal column at the base of which spiritual energy called 'kundalini' lies dormant; in meditation this is used. Obviously ojas cannot be used steadily if it is being frittered away in frequent and excessive sex emotion.

Neither repression nor a weak emasculation is implied in this advice as Vivekananda made clear:

Controlled desire leads to the highest result. Transfer the sexual energy into spiritual energy, but do not emasculate because that is throwing away the power. The stronger this force, the more can be done with it. Only a powerful current of water can do hydraulic mining.

There may be two tragically negative reactions to the insistence on the basis of morality of every kind, not only sexual, as a bedrock for meditation. One is the reaction of, 'Never mind the morality, let's get on with the meditation.' Vivekananda had obviously encountered that one all too frequently, as he made clear:

Here comes Miss So-and-so. She says, 'I am going to be a Yogi.' She tells the news twenty times, meditates fifty days, then she says, 'There is nothing in this religion. I have tried it.' The very basis of spiritual life is not there. The foundation must be the perfect morality. That is the difficulty.

The other, equally destructive reaction, fears the difficulties so strongly that the aspirant does not begin at all. 'If I am expected to be as perfect as *that*, then this is not for me.' That is the same as saying, 'I am cold, so I had better not approach the fire. My health is not perfect, so I will keep away from sunshine and fresh air.' In meditation itself lies the help towards an increasingly great character; the great Self within is stronger than the small ego-self with its self-doubts; what is necessary, as Ramakrishna stressed over and over again, is the longing, the seeking, the sincere determination to succeed. The Christian text, 'Knock, and it shall be opened unto you, seek, and ye shall find', was an expression of his own view, also summed up by Vivekananda: 'You think that you are a small isolated puddle. My friend, you are very much mistaken. Behind you is the infinite ocean of Blessedness.'

(3) *Asana*, or posture.   The posture for meditation should be easy but steady, without muscular tension, and the spinal column should be straight, with head erect. For those who cannot sit cross-legged, a chair of the right height, with feet tucked under the chair to keep the back straight, is equally suitable. 'As a rule, you will find that the spinal column must be left free. It is not intended to bear the weight of the body' (Vivekananda). It is assumed that the aspirant will meditate at least twice a day, preferably in the morning and the evening, if possible before taking food, and certainly not immediately after a heavy meal.

(4) *Pranayama*.   'Prana' is the vital energy in the system. It is the same energy that makes the earth move, the heart beat, and our lungs breathe. Pranayama, generally regarded as breathing control, is in fact control of the prana, the energy which vitalizes the body. Various simple exercises were given by Vivekananda, and can be found in books published by the Order, but in general it is considered much wiser to learn these from a teacher than to practice them alone. It has also been stressed that in deep meditation, the breathing naturally calms down and slows as concentration deepens; so a slowing of the breath, a quiet, even breathing, is sufficient for the beginner who is practising without personal instruction.

(5) *Pratyahara.* This means the gathering in of the forces of the mind, which have become scattered; a withdrawal of the restless mind into calm. We bring with us into meditation time so many concerns, worries, desires, hopes, fears, and often plain idiocies, in our minds, that we feel chained until we can become free of them. This is a universal experience, and yogis accept this fact as the mystics and saints of all religions accept it.

Arjuna (the human soul) says to Krishna (God) in the Bhagavad-Gita, 'Restless man's mind is. How shall he tame it? Truly, I think the wind is no wilder.'

Krishna replies that the mind can be brought under control 'by constant practice, and the use of dispassion.' He also advises, 'Struggling hard, and using the right means.' When a man complained to Ramakrishna that he could not control his mind, Ramakrishna replied, 'Why do you not practise Abhyasa Yoga?' (which means patiently bringing back the mind again and again to the thought of God). There are many ways of 'using the right means'; each of us, in struggling to bring the mind under control, will find a way suitable to our particular nature. But one method strongly advised in the early stages is to let the mind wander as it will. We simply sit and watch where it goes. After a while we become increasingly conscious that something – someone – within us is watching the mind. Then we can say, 'I am not the mind. I am That which is watching it move.' Detachment and dispassion is beginning. As meditation deepens, we find that we have become detached from the body, to some extent; there may be a noise in the road outside, but though our physical ears did presumably hear it, it did not register on the mind; just as in a time of violent emotion or grief, if someone says, 'Did you hear the plane overhead?' we reply, 'What plane? Was there a plane?' The ears, our organs of hearing, acted as usual; but we were for a while detached from them and from the body. It is doubtful if even a sudden physical pain would have reached us in our grief. Ramakrishna always said that one strong emotion pushes out others; make the strong emotion a love for God. This was his constant advice, repeated again and again.

Another great help to us in gathering-in scattered thoughts lies in beginning a detachment from thoughts of our daily duties, relationships and work, for a short while *before* we sit for meditation, as though we are slowly closing a door so that for a while we can be alone with God; and since 'All Is He', we are forgetting

His manifestations in others and in the world, and going to Him – or to That, if we prefer the Impersonal – in pure and undiluted form. If we slam the door of the mind shut too abruptly and expect to hurl ourselves straight into deep concentration, we may find that the mind plays its usual tricks and opens the door again. If anxieties remain, then we can place our loved ones in the care of God, as though we were giving them into the care of a mother, or placing them in healing light; and prayer, not in the sense of asking for some greedy gain for ourselves, but as simply as one would talk to a friend, leads us naturally and gently into meditation.

The continuing light shed by meditation across our daily living helps us here, also, for there is no break in the chain, nothing artificial. If every daily duty, whether it is housework, office work, anything at all that we do, is consciously done in the presence of God; if letters are placed on the meditation table, if we have one, before they are posted; if food is cooked for the Lord; if the mantra or any word which is holy to us flows through the mind as we stand in the bus queue; then we are walking a road which leads straight to meditation. The child who shouted triumphantly as she posted a letter, 'I pushed it right into the box, and I said the mantra', had the right idea. The letter-posting was a ritual as important as lighting a lamp on an altar, and it had to be done properly and purified by the mantra. In later life, meditation would link very naturally with that attitude of mind.

At this stage of meditation the repetition of a mantra is helpful, and some people use a rosary, for the movement of the fingers helps them until the wheel of the mind slows, and then both the movement of the fingers and the repetition of the mantra finally stops. The mantra is a purifying force which sinks from the level of the conscious into the subconscious and works there. It is good to fall asleep at night repeating the mantra in our minds, and its associations with meditation and all that we worship continues to work in our sleep; we may even wake with the mantra still in our minds. This also removes any sense of formality and awe, during meditation, for the mantra is familiar, holy and beloved; awe and formality bring a feeling of separation, and we have finished with separation. We are going towards Wholeness.

(6) *Dharana.*   This is the fixing of the mind upon one spot. In yoga, the object of meditation is regarded as being within the meditator. The mind is concentrated on one of the seven centres

of consciousness, and the centre most suitable (and also advised by Ramakrishna) is the heart; not the physiological heart, but a place imagined as just above the pit of the stomach. It is as though the body were an empty, hollow temple, and the object of worship is visualized as shining within it. After much practice, the centre of meditation sometimes rises to the brain, but it is not wise to start there. It will rise naturally when the time comes, or it may remain in the heart.

There are people who wish to leap straight to the Formless in their meditation; to the Absolute in one leap. A few can do it, but it has been said that those of enormous energy can leap straight to the roof of a house, but it is unwise; it may cause injury, and so stairs are provided. Proceeding up the stairs, it is most natural to centre meditation at first on God with form: in most cases, the form of a human being who has himself attained spiritual freedom; one of the world's great Incarnations or teachers.

A God-realized human being is like a wave in the great ocean of Brahman; the wave has a recognizable form, the ocean itself is as yet too big for us to visualize; we, also with form, are like bubbles on the wave; one day we shall break and become one with the wave, and so, one with the ocean. Over the years, meditation may move naturally to the Formless. When the time comes, the fruit ripens, as Ramakrishna said. We are unlikely to move straight to the heights of samadhi; but the light will become clearer, it will spread across our life, and we are given glimpses along the way. After many years, some may acquire the power to meditate on primal energy, the energy which projects the universe; and eventually we hope to transcend (not to destroy) the ego, in pure Being. The Mother gives each child the food suited to its digestion, said Ramakrishna, and as the child grows the diet may change; and all through life, the food for one may not be the same as the food for another; it is all the same fish, but cooked in different ways.

Harmony is the result of finding and playing perfectly one's own note, one's own theme; what it is will become clear as meditation continues; for this is a lifetime's music.

(7) *Dhyana.* This is next to the super-conscious state, the peace that passes all understanding. It has been likened to the pouring of oil from one vessel to another without a break. The mind flows *direct* towards the object of meditation, without a break. We need not strain or worry; beautifully, naturally, it

happens; for a while everything is forgotten, and we experience more fully than ever before what we truly are.

(8) *Samadhi.* Super-consciousness. There are two types of samadhi : one, Savikalpa samadhi, in which the soul is still conscious of itself in relation with God, the other, Nirvikalpa samadhi, in which there is only pure Consciousness, pure Being.

The eight steps lead to the roof of the house. Ramakrishna taught that though a few great souls may reach the roof and then turn back in compassion to show others the way, *all* the steps are made of the same material as the roof; all that matters is the longing to find the way, and the determination to continue when we have started.

Many religions use mantras, holy words or phrases. In Christianity, 'Our Father', 'Hail Mary', and the Jesus prayer of the Eastern church, 'Lord Jesus Christ, Have Mercy on me'. St Francis, in religious ecstasy, repeated constantly, 'My God and my All'. Jesus often used the word, 'Abba' – Father. A word can have deep spiritual significance, in sound as well as in meaning. 'In the beginning was the Word, and the Word was with God, and the Word was God.'

In yoga, the mantra is regarded as sound Brahman. It is that which protects; the sounds were revealed to the *rishis* in super-conscious state, and the highest is 'Om', which is said to contain all other mantras within itself. The guru initiates a disciple with a mantra suited to that disciple; it usually includes 'Om' and the name of the Chosen Ideal of the disciple, often linked by a seed-word. Those who have no mantra would use 'Om', or any word which is especially holy to them.

Ramakrishna was often asked if a guru was necessary for spiritual progress. He warned seekers very seriously against falling into the clutches of an incompetent teacher.

If the teacher is an 'unripe' one, then the disciple cannot get rid of his ego or of the shackles of the world. . . . Anyone and everyone cannot be a guru. A huge timber floats on the water and can carry many – animals as well. But a piece of worthless wood sinks, if a man sits on it, and drowns him. Therefore in every age God incarnates himself as the guru, to teach humanity. Satchidananda alone is the guru . . . and the [true] guru is the thread that leads to God.

He did not say that progress is impossible without a guru, but he taught that a true guru is of immense spiritual help to the seeker. Satchidananda is the 'guru nature' within each of us, and in an advanced spiritual state the mind itself acts as guru; but where possible, 'If a man in the form of a guru awakens spiritual consciousness in you, then know for certain that it is God the Absolute who has assumed the human form for your sake.'

The tests of a true guru are certainly very demanding. Traditionally, he must not only be 'versed in the scriptures' but live in their spirit; he must be Brahmanistham (established in Brahman); he must be Akamahata – unsmitten by desire – unmotivated by selfish purpose, and never demand money. Also, he will avoid name and fame – no publicity-seeking, no egotism. He must be open, guileless, free from deceit. He should be a celibate, unentangled in family life or property, for unless he has snapped his own chains of attachment, he cannot guide the disciple. But if he is celibate and still full of worldly anxieties and desires, then he cannot himself have reached a stage where he can be a 'ripe' guru. Such a one is rare; but better none, said Ramakrishna, then the dangers of a false guru.

And when the disciple is ready with the prayer and longing for truth which, like the first streaks of dawn in the sky, show that sunrise is approaching, nothing can stop the rising of the sun. The guru will be found; and the guru himself will find his true disciples.

Whether the guru has been found or not, the advice regarding the time, place and general setting of the meditation period, is practical and specific. In Indian houses, a special room was kept for meditation; today, especially in the West, this is often out of the question. Ramakrishna advised 'a corner of the room' if necessary, and in small houses in the West, it is always possible to keep one place, however small – even if only a few feet square – as a quiet place; possibly a corner of a bedroom. The operative word is 'keep'.

If the meditation place is kept inviolate, which is perhaps a highly coloured word to indicate the simple fact that it is never used for any other purpose, no everyday parcels, shopping bags, brushes or combs are allowed there, no books other than those suitable and helpful, and family arguments and discussions are kept well away from it; then the meditation place – whether it consists of a chair and table, a mat, a shelf before which the meditator sits – becomes in time a place of peace and tranquillity where at times of stress one can go simply for a few moments' stillness and peace. Before leaving the house one can visit it, and again on return; it becomes a centre, a focal point, and its associations are deeply important.

The spiritual nature of each one of us, leads us to make of our meditation place whatever will help us most. To some, pictures, flowers, and the burning of incense may be as helpful as a stark simplicity, with one picture, or none at all, may be for others. There is no hard and fast rule. Since it is usually helpful to begin with a short reading from whatever book is holy to us, a book or books may well be kept there. However simple, or however colourful, the meditation place should be kept scrupulously clean.

The God-realized saint may be able to meditate anywhere; we ourselves may find that meditation in other places becomes easier as time goes on; but we are not making a fetish of a meditation place, we are simply giving ourselves a geographical centre, a spiritual home, a place to which we can go; and if we were suddenly forced to leave home and live in a cave we should probably instinctively make our own meditation place in it again. A prisoner in his cell may put up pictures of pop stars, or a photograph of his wife and children, or perhaps a crucifix; instinctively he is making a small corner that is his alone, where he may express whatever he likes, where he achieves his own privacy. Pictures which are obscene, pictures which are holy, pictures which may show a beloved garden or a sandy beach a thousand miles away where the waves still break on shores that the prisoner can never see : who are we to say what will express human longing in a place of one's own? A prison may express many things.

In meditation, holiness, joy, peace, tranquillity, and strength; how we express these – what is helpful, what is hindrance – this we instinctively find for ourselves. We are *not* in a prison! We are in a temple, in the home of the spirit. We are advised to wash our hands and face before meditation if it occurs at a time of day where a complete bath is impractical. It is surprising how helpful this psychological washing away of life's dust, expressed in physical washing, can be.

If this is the place, what is the time? Ideally, the time when night passes into day, and day into night. The traditional periods are dawn and dusk, and also noon; but we do not live in a traditional world where this is always possible. Again, each must do what suits him best; if the busy office worker facing rush-hour traffic finds early morning meditation impossible, he will probably sit quietly in his meditation place for a short while, to read, to pray, to direct his thoughts, to dedicate himself; for him the evening may be a better time for deep meditation. To a mother, the quiet of the house after children have gone to school and her husband to work, may be better than early morning when the family clamours for her attention. What matters is that the meditation times should be as fixed and constant as possible, so that our spiritual lives move in a steady rhythm. Sometimes we are especially in a mood for meditation; we should seize this mood when it comes and ride the crest of the wave, for there is an ebb and flow in the spiritual life. But when we feel no desire for meditation, still we should persist; Ramakrishna himself said that on some days he felt great spiritual awakening, on others he did not; what matters is the steady persistence. Heavy food should not be taken before meditation; on the other hand, fatigue and hunger can bring nervous irritability. The less food before meditation the better; but when a Western disciple of Vivekananda's admitted that she could not face morning meditation without drinking a cup of tea first, and asked if this would impede her spiritual progress, Vivekananda replied that he wouldn't think much of a religion that could be ruined by a cup of tea.

The time of meditation is the time for leaving the ego behind, of forgetting our small selves; the first step is often a short period in which we send out thoughts of peace and goodwill to all creation, animate and inanimate, to all creatures great and small, for all are moving towards God, and will attain Him in due course. A similar current of peace and goodwill is sent to all those we know, love and care for; including those we do not like or who may dislike us.

We are sitting erect, with head, neck and chest in a straight line, breathing slowly and rhythmically, and in our minds we bow down to whatever is the God of our own conception, and we salute all these great ones who have come to shed light and peace on the earth throughout the ages, whether of our own religion or not.

At this point there is usually an offering of ourselves in dedication, and a prayer for peace and light; a spontaneous opening of the mind and spirit in complete naturalness. It must be remembered that these are only suggestions; each spirit will take from them what is needed. This opens the way; now as we begin to repeat the mantra, the first steps are taken; meditation will begin.

II

The different types of meditation will vary with each individual, and all that can be given here are one or two examples which will illustrate how each meditation is in fact leading to the same point. Since all examples originated with the teachings of Ramakrishna and Vivekananda, or were approved by them, let us first consider their own words on the subject of meditation. When addressing an audience in America, in 1900, Vivekananda said:

When the mind is doubtful, that is not its great state. Its great state is meditation. It looks upon things and sees things, not identifying itself with anything else. As long as I feel pain, I have identified myself with the body. When I feel joy or pleasure, I have identified myself with the body. But the high state will look with the same blissfulness upon pleasure or upon pain. . . . Every meditation is direct super-consciousness. In perfect concentration the soul becomes actually free from the bonds of the gross body and knows itself as it is. . . .

All our fears, all worries, anxieties, troubles, mistakes, weakness, evil, are from that one great blunder – that we are bodies. . . . In India, two persons meet. In English they say, 'How do you do?' The Indian greeting is, 'Are you upon yourself?' The moment you stand upon something else, you run the risk of being miserable. That is what I mean by meditation – the soul trying to stand upon itself. That state must surely be the healthiest state of the soul, when it is thinking of itself, residing in its own glory. . . .

The whole of the universe has been demonstrated into one. That science is called the science of Vedanta. The whole universe is one. The one runs through all this seeming variety. . . .

We all struggle – if we cannot reach the Absolute, we will get somewhere, and it will be better than we are now. Meditation consists in this practice of dissolving everything into the Ultimate Reality – spirit.

. . . The Kingdom of Heaven is within us. . . . Realize yourself. That is all there is to do. Know yourself as you are – infinite spirit.

In the words of Ramakrishna:

Think of the sun and of ten jars filled with water. The sun is reflected in each jar. At first you see the real sun and ten reflected ones. If you break nine of the jars, there will remain only the real sun and one reflection. Each jar represents a jiva [soul]. Following the reflection one can find the real sun. Through the individual soul one can reach the Supreme Soul. Through spiritual discipline the individual soul can get the vision of the Supreme Soul. What remains when the last jar is broken cannot be described.

He also said, 'In the beginning of meditation the objects of the senses appear before the aspirant. But when the meditation becomes deep, they no longer bother him. They are left outside.'

He often used the illustration of a flow of oil, in which many drops of oil become one unending and unbroken stream, when oil is poured from one vessel to another. 'Do you know what one feels in meditation? The mind becomes like a continuous flow of oil – it thinks of one object, and one object only, and that object is God. It does not think of anything else.'

The meditation which is natural to the jnani, the meditation upon the Absolute, will obviously differ from the approach of the bhakta who turns his mind towards personal God.

Ramakrishna said :

There are two kinds of meditation, one on the formless God and the other on God with form. But meditation on the formless God is extremely difficult. In that meditation you must wipe out all that you see or hear. You contemplate only the nature of Your Inner Self.

This aspirant is seeking the infinity of the spirit, the Void beyond all forms and attributes. He is aiming for spiritual Knowledge and Freedom, and it is a path especially suited for monastics or those withdrawn from the world. Pure Consciousness is not an idea or an abstraction, but a Reality. It is man's deathless Self, the core of his being. The form of meditation can also begin by meditating on 'God with attributes' if necessary. The steps lead to the roof. The idea of Freedom, and of space – not space as we understand it, but the ultimate Space which is in the soul – was illustrated by Ramakrishna in reference to possible forms of meditation of this kind. In the early stages of meditation, visualizing plays an important part.

In referring to the meditation of a jnani, Ramakrishna said :

Everywhere is water; all the regions above and below are filled with water; man, like a fish, is swimming joyously in that water. In real meditation you will actually see all this . . . Do you know another

way a jnani meditates? Think of infinite akasa [space] and a bird
flying there, joyfully spreading its wings . . . its joy is limitless.

He described also how he had meditated on the flame of a
lamp, visualizing first its outer colour and then finally its centre;
an unmoving flame in a windless place.

A form of meditation sometimes described by Vivekananda,
and more suitable for those with enquiring and perhaps more
scientific minds than those who prefer simplicity, contemplates
the sushumna and the kundalini lying like a serpent coiled at the
base of the spine, ready to rise to the brain. In explicit description and even with drawings he described what was happening as
meditation proceeded; this is helpful to some but not to others,
just as one woman may be helped by studying the physical facts
of childbirth while another may be repelled by anatomical
details; all that matters is the successful bearing of a healthy
child.

Meditation upon God with form is concentrated on the centre
of consciousness in the body of the meditator known as 'the heart',
not in the head, as is the case with the jnani. This does not refer
to the physiological heart, but a place imagined as just above the
pit of the stomach. As in the earlier illustration, where the jnani
moves away from his body – and, in a sense, deifies it – by thinking only of limitless space or water, and the bird or fish joyously
sporting there in freedom; so in the meditation of the bhakta,
the body is thought of as though it were an empty, hollow temple,
and the Ishta – possibly an Incarnation of God – whichever
Chosen Ideal is worshipped – is visualized as seated, shining within it. A beautiful symbolism may be used; the lotus closes its
petals at night and the flower droops. In the light of the morning,
it becomes erect and the petals open to the light. So, as meditation begins, the lotus of the heart (described as red and eight-
petalled) opens and blooms. It is sometimes visualized as holding
the sun within it, within the sun is the moon, within the moon is
fire, and within the fire is seated the Chosen Ideal, the object of
meditation. The Ishta is seen as seated, radiant, loving, serene
and blissful; he is translucent. First his form is visualized, then
his face, and lastly his spiritual heart, the centre of the light;
until finally the meditator is meditating upon this great heart, the
heart of an illumined and totally pure soul, *within* his own heart.
Here, as in the meditation on the flame of the lamp, one goes

from a larger figure to a smaller, so that concentration narrows down to a point. In all these meditations, one is not seeking to 'think about' but to *become* the object of meditation; to strip away body and mind until one becomes what in fact one *is*. The bird hopping on the branches of the tree of life ceases to eat the sweet and bitter fruits for a while, and becomes for a time at least, the radiant, serene, and deathless golden bird who stands forever at the top of the tree. When the meditator returns to daily living, he should take the light with him, so that he is conscious of its illumination throughout the day. 'You will be doing your duties,' said Ramakrishna, 'but let that pleasant intoxication remain with you.'

A form of meditation which is helpful to those who are more drawn to the abstract, especially those to whom sound is important, is meditation on the simple ultimate sound – the Pranava, or Om. Om pervades all sounds or words, and is sound – Brahman. The Mandukya Upanishad divides Om into 'AUM' and 'Amatra', which is the silent aspect of the sound. AUM represent, in each letter, waking, dreaming and deep sleep. The Amatra stands for the Self, who witnesses these three states, who is eternal, and can never be fully represented by a word; the Self we find in meditation. While repeating 'Om', the meditator imagines that the Self within his body is like the latent heat-energy in wood and by meditating on Om he is going to light up the fire of Self-Knowledge within himself.

He thinks that Om is going to every nerve, every muscle, every breath of the body – even the emotions and thought. All thoughts must be holy. Another meditation on Om is given in the Mandaka Upanishad. Here Om is the bow and meditation is the act of shooting the arrow. The mind is the arrow. The mind is placed in Om and pointed to the target. This helps the one-pointed mind travel directly to pure consciousness, which is the meditator's true Self.

Everything in this meditation, merges in Om; the noise of a car, a jet, any disturbing sound, all becomes Om and is included in the meditation. All content of the mind becomes Om. There will only be Om, the Anahata (unstruck) primal spiritual vibration. At last that vibration also will merge into the ultimate silence of the Self.

Meditation is a very personal and private thing; it is noticeable how often 'M' in his book, *The Gospel of Sri Ramakrishna*, simply comments, 'then the Master gave the disciple some instruction on meditation'; he does not set out Ramakrishna's words and instruction, as he does on every other subject. What passes between guru and disciple is not a matter for public discussion.

But by considering here, in very general form and very simply, one or two methods of meditation (for Ramakrishna and Vivekananda were extremely firm in their teachings that in general terms there must be nothing hidden or esoteric), we can see that all meditations vary according to the nature of the meditator, but they all have certain essentials in common.

Since the meditator is going beyond the body and mind to dwell for a while in his true and eternal Self, that Self which will not die at death, when body and mind are left behind; so in all these forms of meditation, the body becomes first a cleansed and purified receptacle – air or water in which the bird or fish goes free; the lamp holding the flame; the temple in which the personal God dwells, until his heart is realized within the meditator's own heart; the dissolving of all into Om – in every case the body is purified and the mind is brought to a fine point, and then both are left behind. What happens then, as Ramakrishna said, cannot be described. But even a few steps in the right direction will bring us greater peace than we have ever known.

At the end of meditation, the meditation is offered up to Him – or That – whom we worship; and it may be offered up for the good of all, for every created being or thing; not for our own small ego-self. Ramakrishna taught that what we find in ourselves, we find in others also. In meditation we draw apart, we put the world and our own bodies and minds away from us. The musician can only create a harmony if he creates it in his own instrument and concentrates on that. Then he finds that the whole orchestra is playing, and his music is a part of the whole. He finds that all music comes from the same source, and he must find that source in himself, for without it he can only create disharmony. Said Ramakrishna :

The nearer you come to God, the more you feel peace. Peace, peace, peace – Supreme peace ! The nearer you come to the Ganges, the more you feel its coolness; you will feel completely soothed when you plunge into the river.

And the whole essence of meditation is summed up in these words of Vivekananda :

Excepting the infinite spirit, everything else is changing. There is the whirl of change. Permanence is nowhere except in yourself. *There* is the infinite joy, unchanging. Meditation is the gate that opens that to us. . . . In the long run the power of meditation separates ourselves from the body, and then the soul knows itself as it is – the unborn, the deathless, the birthless Being.

9

HARMONY OF THE FOUR YOGAS; AND HARMONY WITHIN MAN'S NATURE

Ramakrishna did not found a sect, or a religion; indeed, he was sometimes worried lest the brilliance and energy of Vivekananda should lead *him* into founding a sect. As Vivekananda said of him, 'He did not come to trumpet his own name. He *was* that great life.' He lived, and left it to others to explain and to carry forward what he himself lived out and gave to individuals who came to him. The fact that he was unique in achieving the heights of spiritual Realization through all the yogas, through the practice of several religions (including Christianity) and experienced the same heights through all of them; this did not lessen his simplicity, his loving compassion, or his sense of humour; they all rested on an iron ground-work of renunciation, self-discipline and strength. It began to become clear that a stream of spirituality was going to flow from him across the world, but it was not to be a stream that wrenched people off their own course and put them on to another; he came not to destroy but to fulfil.

Vivekananda said of him :

His principle was, first form character, first earn spirituality, and results will come of themselves. His favourite illustration was, 'When the lotus opens the bees come of their own accord to seek the honey; so let the lotus of your character be full-blown, and the results will follow.' That is a great lesson to learn.

. . . For years I lived with that man, but never did I hear those lips utter one word of condemnation for any sect. He had the same sympathy for all sects; he had found the harmony between them.

A man may be intellectual, or devotional, or mystic, or active; the various religions represent one or the other of these types. Yet it is possible to combine all the four in one man, and this is what future humanity is going to do. That was his idea. He condemned no one, but saw the good in all.

The idea of encouraging the harmony within each person by developing all four yogas within each man and woman, gained strength in Vivekananda's thinking as he travelled in the West and throughout India.

The teaching of this new Incarnation or Teacher, Ramakrishna, is that the best points of Yoga, Devotion, Knowledge and Work [Raja Yoga, Bhakti, Jnana and Karma Yoga] must be combined now so as to form a new society.

Now a religion, to satisfy the largest proportion of mankind, must be able to supply food for all these various types of minds; and where this capability is wanting the existing sects all become one-sided.

. . . Religion must be able to show how to realize the philosophy that teaches us that this world is one, that there is but one Existence in the universe. . . . Similarly, if the mystic comes, we must welcome him, be ready to give him the science of mental analysis and practically demonstrate it before him. And if emotional people come, we must 'drink the cup of love and become mad.' If the energetic worker comes we must work with him, with all the energy we have. And this combination will be the ideal of the nearest approach to a universal religion. Would to God that all men were so constituted that in their minds *all* these elements, of philosophy, mysticism, emotion and of work were equally present in full. That is my ideal, my ideal of a perfect man. Everyone who has only one or two of these elements in his character, I consider 'one-sided' and this world is almost full of such 'one-sided' men, with knowledge of that one road only in which *they* move; and anything else is dangerous and horrible to them.

It was the egotistic forcing of one's own ideal, one's own spiritual nature, on others, which he regarded as so dangerous. The vice of 'Only *my* watch tells the correct time', as Ramakrishna called it. The four elements making up the four yogas are in all of us, usually with one or two stronger than the others; Vivekananda regarded the harmony within each of us as a blending of all four, but it did not stop there. Having found our own harmony, this naturally leads us to fellowship with those we meet, and we can respond to the spiritual traits in them which are in us also. We may, for instance, be more bhakta than jnani, but when we meet the jnani, there is enough of the philosopher in each of us to make recognition and brotherhood possible.

The harmony of these four yogas within each one of us also safeguards our own spiritual development, as he pointed out. Philosophy and discrimination will stop love and devotion from becoming sentimental or fanatical; love will prevent philosophy from becoming dry and remote; work burns away the ego, and meditation is the light that surrounds and protects our life, the light that leads us forward.

And this religion is attained by what we, in India, call Yoga-union. To the worker, it is union between men and the whole of humanity; to the mystic, between his lower and higher Self; to the lover, union between himself and the God of Love; and to the philosopher it is the union of *all* existence. That is what is meant by Yoga.

To illustrate this harmony of the four yogas, Vivekananda introduced a symbol which has become the symbol of the Ramakrishna movement, printed on all the books published by the Order, shown on the gate or front door of the Ramakrishna Centres, familiar in every place where the humanitarian work, or the teaching, meditation and fellowship of the movement is known.

The symbol is a circle. In the centre is a swan, representing the supreme soul or great Self. The swan floats on water (often rough water, as Vivekananda pointed out) which is work, Karma Yoga. Bhakti Yoga is represented by a lotus in the foreground, and behind the swan, is the sun – which is Jnana Yoga, the Yoga of Knowledge. The whole picture is surrounded and enclosed by a snake; this reminds us of the kundalini, the 'coiled serpent' at the base of the spine which rises in meditation; the snake is meditation; Raja Yoga encircles and completes the picture.

To this harmony of the four great yogas within us, must be added another harmony without which chaos may still threaten us. It is a teaching in-built into Indian religious thought, but less familiar to the West.

The teaching concerns the three 'gunas'. The three gunas are the essence of maya. They are not separable from one another and are always changing. Everything in the universe consists of these three : 'sattva', 'rajas' and 'tamas'. Guna also means a rope; the gunas are sometimes referred to as three strands. They are the strands, or ropes, which bind us to the wheel of continual reincarnation.

Within the character of man, tamas is the lowest; it represents what is dark, inert, or evil. Rajas is higher; rajas implies great activity, though sometimes of an egotistic sort; never the less, rajas helps the soul to struggle and fight clear of tamas, before we can proceed to sattva, which is the highest. Sattva demonstrates the noble qualities : serenity, compassion, love, strength, humility, unselfishness, and so on.

It is emphasized that one cannot jump straight from tamas to sattva. The great activity of rajas must come first, but often brings with it a certain restlessness, a tendency to show off, which has not reached the quiet humility of sattva yet, but is on the way. Ramakrishna, in talking to a sub-judge who was visiting him, was very amusing in his account of the three types of people who are totally expressing one or other of the three gunas.

The characteristics of sattva, rajas, and tamas are very different. Egotism, excessive sleep, gluttony, lust, anger and the like are traits of people with tamas. Men with rajas entangle themselves in many activities. Such a man has clothes all spick and span. His house is immaculately clean. A portrait of the Queen [Victoria] hangs on a wall in his drawing-room. When he worships God he wears a silk cloth. He has a string of rudraksha beads around his neck, and in between the beads he puts a few gold ones. When someone comes to visit the worship hall in his house, he himself acts as guide. After showing the hall, he says to the visitor, 'Please come this way sir. There are other things too – the floor of white marble and the nat-mandir with its exquisite carvings.' When he gives in charity, he makes a show of it. But a man endowed with sattva is quiet and peaceful. So far as dress is concerned, anything will do. He earns enough money to give his stomach the simplest of food; he never flatters men to get money. . . . He does not hanker for name and fame. His worship, charity and meditation are all done in secret; people do not know about them at all . . . sattva is the last step of the stairs; next is the roof. As soon as sattva is acquired there is no delay in reaching God. One step forward, and God is realized.

These three gunas exist in some proportion in us all, though the people Ramakrishna refers to are mainly dominated by one of the gunas in each case. Regarding the three as they exist to some extent in us all, it is interesting to see that all three – even sattva, the highest – are known as 'binding-ropes' or 'robbers'. A story which he often told, concerned three robbers; tamas, rajas and sattva. Tamas attacked a man and tried to kill him, for tamas destroys. Rajas, the second robber, was a little better. He bound him tightly instead. Sattva unbound the ropes, took him by the hand and led him home. But when the man reached home and begged sattva to enter, sattva replied, 'I too am a robber; I can lead you home, but I cannot come in. You must enter alone.'

F

This may at first appear surprising. One who is totally sattvic may be what the West would call a saint; certainly somebody of great goodness. But the truly great and good man may be tied by his own goodness; he may even fall into that subtle trap which lies in wait for the saint; he may become conscious of his own goodness, and even, subconsciously, just a little proud of it. Pure sattva is not self-conscious at all; the man who is ready to 'enter the house alone' does good without thinking about it, quite unself-consciously, as a flower gives off perfume. It has become quite natural. But while we are struggling, we need not worry about reaching such an advanced state that even sattva holds us back. When we reach *that* stage, sattva has brought us to the door of the house, and, as Ramakrishna said, 'One step forward, and God is realized.'

How, then, do we make a harmony of these three, which exist in us all, in greater or lesser degree? It is fascinating to see how the various schools of modern psychology also teach that we have these varying tendencies in our nature. They give all three different names, but the same idea is there. And they advise us to make a harmony by *using* these three; which is exactly what Rama-krishna himself advised.

Sattva could easily lack energy; sattva, however calm and serene, must be full of vitality; and it can draw this from rajas. 'As long as sattva exists,' said Ramakrishna, 'it calls on rajas for help, and rajas can get help from tamas.'

The help which rajas can get from tamas is obviously toughness and even, when it is necessary, a certain aggression. Rajas can degenerate into tamas: 'It is the very nature of rajas to involve a man in many worldly activities. That is why rajas degenerates into tamas.' If that is so, then how can tamas help? Ramakrishna often advised those with a strong tamasic streak to use force in tamasic Bhakti; almost to pound with their fists on God, as in a parable he told of the child who pesters the mother and pulls at her skirt for attention, until she gives him the coin to buy a toy she has previously denied to him ('Cry – clinging Heaven by the hems'). Jesus made exactly the same point; it occurs in the teach-ings of many of religion's great teachers. To quote Ramakrishna:

A man endowed with tamasic Bhakti has burning faith. Such a devotee literally extorts boons from God, even as a robber falls upon a man and plunders his money. . . . If you can give a spiritual turn to your tamas, you can realize God with its help. Force your demands on God. He is by no means a stranger to you. He is indeed your very own.

The child has a right to make demands on the parent, who is 'his very own'. So, all the gunas can be used in the great harmony; and, in the end, sattva will lead us home. One step more – leaving even sattva behind – and we are there.

Lastly, we come to the question which every seeker, entangled in the world and its duties and involvements, put to Ramakrishna. The question came up again and again; it always has, and it always will. For those who have accepted all this, or as much of it as they can as yet assimilate; for earnest seekers who are struggling on the path but who cannot become monks, nuns, or renunciates (for, as Ramakrishna said, it is no use shaking the melon from the tree until it is ripe; when it is ripe, it will come away naturally), meanwhile – what is the way? In this chaotic world, what is the way?

The first great advice, as we have seen, is to increase one's longing restlessness, yearning; if it is at first only a flicker, that is a beginning; pray, increase it.

One must have for God the yearning of a child. The child sees nothing but confusion when his mother is away. You may try to cajole him by putting a sweetmeat in his hand; but he will not be fooled. He only says, 'No. I want to go to my mother.' . . . And to him alone, the Mother comes running, leaving all Her other duties.

And how of the ego, that 'rogue' as Ramakrishna called it, which trips us up so often, causes such disharmony? We think we have conquered it – and then as he said, it grows up again. So if it must remain, let it remain as 'the ripe ego' was his advice. The ego of servant to master, friend to friend, parent to child, lover to lover – a relationship with God; or, if we are on the way to Non-Dualism, then we are a part of Him; He is enshrined in our hearts in meditation; we can serve Him in all creatures; we are using a 'ripe ego'; it remains, but in humility, and deified.

But how shall we regard this world, in the brief spell we are here? Many were the homely parables and illustrations he gave in answer to that question. Be like the man from the country who visits Calcutta; first he finds a place to stay, and then he is free to roam about the city. Be like the mother turtle who lays her eggs in the sand; she swims out to sea, but her thoughts are on

her unhatched babes. Be like the servant girl who works in a
rich man's house; she regards it as home, and becomes fond of
the people in it; she refers to it as 'our house' and calls her master's
son 'My Hari' – but in her heart she knows that her real home
is in her native village, her own family, perhaps her own child,
is there. One day she will go, but for the moment she identifies her
life with that of the household where she is staying; never forgetting
in her mind that her life is lived in one place, but her true home
is in another.

In this lies the resolution of that greatest of all paradoxes.

On the one hand, all these illustrations point clearly to the
idea that we are aliens, in part identifying our lives with the life
we are now living on this very difficult planet, and yet in our
hearts constantly turning towards God, towards That – our true
and eternal home.

And yet, on the other side of the same coin, we have the great
truth which Ramakrishna experienced fully in his super-conscious state, and which we as yet 'see in a glass darkly, but then
face to face'; we can certainly think along this line and experience it in our own way, as far as we are yet able to do so. And
this truth tells us that we walk in a world in which 'all is That'
or 'All is He'; in which everything, including ourselves, is an
expression of That which we are all consciously or unconsciously,
seeking. In Ramakrishna's words : 'One must love all. No one is
a stranger. It is Hari [God] alone who dwells in all beings. Nothing
exists without Him.'

In that sense – and *only* in that sense – it is true to say that in
this life we are at home. And this is the harmony of the two
apparently opposing truths; that it is only when we turn continually towards our true home in God, to the God who is within us
and within all, and see the world as temporary and alien, that we
find in the end that there is no place where He is not. 'Nothing
exists without Him.'

10

HARMONY OF RELIGIONS

The harmony between a worship of God as personal or impersonal, the harmony between the different aspects of man's nature as shown in the yogas, the harmony that can be made of the gunas, and of our daily workaday life and our spiritual life; all these are a part of the inner life of each one of us. But one of the contributions towards religious experience and thinking for which Ramakrishna himself, Vivekananda, and the Order and the whole movement which he founded, have become best known, is the harmony of religions. If you ask an observer who has seen something of the work of the movement, but who has not studied the experience and thinking on which it all rests, what he regarded as its major contribution, he would probably reply that it was the blending of the meditative and contemplative life of the practical work and humanitarian service of mankind, and he might find the same harmony in the lives of those connected with it. If he did not, then he would probably agree that at the very least all were striving towards it. He would certainly have caught the note, the tone, of the harmony, at any rate in its outward manifestations. Then he would undoubtedly mention the harmony of religions and of philosophies and sects; but the modern emphasis on toleration and ecumenism in the West, excellent though it is and however hopeful may be its development, does not entirely cover all that is meant by the word 'harmony'.

The teaching of Ramakrishna stated clearly that all religions are simply different paths to the same goal of super-consciousness, that they are in fact all one great religion (or one great experience, if the word 'religion' suggests too definite a commitment to a dogma) manifesting itself in various ways, to suit different temperaments, different races, different circumstances. This goes a great deal further than 'toleration'. He also believed that all teachers, prophets, and Incarnations teach essentially the same truths; they, like the religions and philosophies themselves, are manifestations of Brahman, illuminating our path on our journey through maya. 'The Avatara [Incarnation] is always one and the same. Plunging into the ocean of life, he rises up in one place and is known as Krishna; diving again and rising elsewhere, he is known as Christ.'

He taught that each one of us should stand absolutely firm in his own faith, but that the bigotry which insists that 'only *my* watch tells the correct time' is the result of spiritual ignorance. Certainly there may be errors in all spiritual paths, and some paths may appear to us to be better than others; but in time any errors in the paths will become clear to those who walk on them : 'God Himself will help'. It is not for us to drag someone who is sincerely following his own path, on to our own path, or to assume that nothing exists outside our own experience and belief. He told a parable of a small frog who lived in a well, and who became infuriated with a visiting frog who tried to explain to him that the sea was a little bigger than his well. The mere idea that anyone should live in a place different from his own – and still worse, that he should suggest that it might be bigger – so maddened him that he kicked the visiting frog out of his well and remained in contented bigotry, convinced that in his well, and there only, all water was contained.

It is interesting that the metaphor used here is one concerning water. Ramakrishna often used water as a metaphor for the Ultimate, for Brahman, for Satchidananda. Perhaps some of his most often-quoted words are these :

Truth is one; only It is called by different names. All people are seeking the same Truth; the variance is due to climate, temperament, and name. A lake has many ghats [bathing-places]. From one ghat the Hindus take water in jars and call it 'jal'. From another ghat the Mussalmans take water in leather bags and call it 'pani'. From a third the Christians take the same thing and call it 'water'. Suppose someone says that the thing is not 'jal' but 'pani', or that it is not 'water' but 'jal'. It would indeed be ridiculous. But this very thing is at the root of the friction among sects, their misunderstandings and quarrels. This is why people injure and kill one another and shed blood, in the name of religion. But this is not good. Everyone is going toward God. They will all realize Him if they have sincerity and longing of heart.

Here he brings us back to the point he made so often : the need for sincerity; the need for longing.

As for a comparison between religions, certainly some may

seem to us to be nobler, more 'spiritually adult' than others.

But, as he pointed out, the father of many children does not love the baby of his family any the less, because as yet he can only call his father 'Da' or 'Ba', whereas his grown-up son can call him 'Father' and speak to him with more understanding, as an adult. They are at different stages of development, that is all.

For very many centuries in India the various approaches to religion and philosophy have been studied, and it was accepted that there were three possible standpoints which could be taken. These correspond to what in Western terms we call the partisan, the eclectic and the synthetic. The partisan, like the frog in the well, loves his own religion but refuses to consider the possible truth of any others. This may lead to fervour and sincerity; it may also lead to savage fanaticism and blind bigotry.

The eclectic viewpoint is totally different: it is broad-minded and generous, it studies all religions and sees the pure gold running through them all, and it tends to take all the finest spiritual truths or practices from each religion, and blend them together.

This, however, has its dangers. Like all broad-minded and liberal thinking, it may tend to become vague and woolly. It may lack intensity. And, in the end, a definite spiritual path has to be followed. The eclectic sometimes draws together the teachings of many different religions, and makes yet another sect from the result. And this sect will lack the centuries of discipline and achievement, the support and teaching of past great souls, which any one of the religions may have. A player may appreciate, or even play, many instruments; but in the end he must perfect his performance on one instrument. As Ramakrishna said, many paths may lead to Calcutta, and at first one may ask the way from several people, or even try several paths; but when one has found the best path (for himself), he may give a friendly glance to those travelling on other paths, he will see that all roads lead to Calcutta, but he should not keep changing from one path to another, or make a mixture and confusion of the route. He should stay on his own chosen path.

The third approach is synthesis or harmony; perhaps the word 'harmonious' conveys this approach better than 'synthetic'; in fact, it makes a synthesis of the differing creeds, philosophies and faiths. Its aim is unity in diversity; it avoids any attempt at uniformity. It does not exclude or reject; but it does not standardize.

Previously, in India as elsewhere, through the centuries, various philosophies' approaches and schools of thought had sometimes clashed. But gradually the attitude of synthesis and harmony prevailed. The various 'Chosen Ideals' of the Tantras came to be looked upon as manifestations of the one supreme Brahman; the six systems of philosophy were taken as studies of the one Reality from various points of view; and the three schools of Vedanta were finally regarded as so many views of God in Personal and Impersonal aspects, differing because they were seen from different levels of spiritual attainment.

A well-known Hindu hymn says,

May Hari, the Ruler of the three worlds, worshipped by the Shaivites as Shiva, by the Vedantins as Brahman, by the Buddhists as the Buddha, by the followers of Nyaya as the Chief Agent, by the Jains as the Liberated, and by the Karmakandins as the Principle of Law, grant our prayers.

This reconciliation of the Indian sects, paths and philosophies is simply and beautifully expressed in the words which Hindu boys are taught to utter at the conclusion of their morning and evening prayers: 'All adoration leads to God, just as all water that descends from the heavens wends its way to the sea.'

Two great teachers of synthesis and harmony carried the teachings further: Guru Nanak and Kabir. In the nineteenth century came Raja Ram Mohan Roy, who advocated the adoration of One Universal Spirit – and Keshab Chandra Sen, a well-known Brahmo, who was a friend of Ramakrishna. Ramakrishna reconciled all religions, sects and paths of the modern world, not only those that were Indian. His unique contribution was the actual experiencing of the various states described, and his discovery by experience and not by theory that the same super-conscious state could be achieved through the worship of other Chosen Ideals as well as those that were Indian (Jesus, among others) and by adopting the totally different attitudes of mind, approach to life, and disciplines of many different paths. He achieved the heights of Nirvikalpa samadhi through deep love of a personal God – usually associated with the Vaishnavites – just as he did through the total renunciation of the personal, on the path of Shankara; these two are generally regarded as opposite extremes of the spiritual spectrum. But, having experienced for himself, he never the less taught his followers, 'Fix your mind on one thing only, either the Personal God or the Impersonal God.'

The super-conscious states he achieved fascinated the curious or the scientific; the suspension of breathing and heart-beat, the apparent cessation of all functions; the 'becoming' in bliss in which he had to be supported in case he should fall; the constant passing into this state, from the laughter and teaching of his everyday life, or in the agony of his final illness; he dwelt, as he said, on the borders of the ephemeral and the eternal and passed from one to another.

But he himself regarded this as less important than the formation of character. It is possible to achieve – or even to imitate – apparently mystical physical states and to return from them with no advancement in spirituality at all. Such was the character he achieved, and the spirituality felt so strongly by all who met him, that just to remain in his presence for a while was regarded by many people as giving them more than a lifetime's philosophy could do.

His loving, childlike spirit and total absence of egotism, his imparting to all who came to him everything that he had to give, even when the pain of throat cancer made talking almost impossible; it was this that caught – and held – his disciples. Like Jesus, he thought little of miracles, and preferred that anything he did which appeared miraculous to some people, should not be regarded as important, or advertised.

Vivekananda had been taught by Ramakrishna that he should not 'trumpet his Master's name', which might cause the formation of one more sect. In later years, the publication of 'M' 's *Gospel Of Sri Ramakrishna* and other books by those who had known him and recorded his words and their memories of him, brought many people to learn from Ramakrishna as a teacher, or to worship him as an Incarnation of God, or to follow him in whatever way was natural to them. The Hindu belief in the 'Chosen Ideal' by which the Incarnation, prophet, or great soul is chosen by the devotee by a natural spiritual attraction, not by 'conversion', in which allegiance to him is not taught or demanded as part of acceptance of his teachings, seemed unusual to many people in the West. But Vivekananda believed that those who were to come to Ramakrishna, would come; what mattered first was to bring his teachings. So in his lecture tours in America and England, before the life and gospel of Ramakrishna was written, the only lectures he gave about Ramakrishna – one in New York, and one in England, both in 1896 – were subsequently combined under the title of 'My Master'. And here we have the words, often touching in their simplicity, of one who had known and loved the man, and who had come to bring his message to the world.

First make character – that is the highest duty that you can perform. Know Truth for yourself, and there will be many to whom you can teach it afterwards; they will all come. This was the attitude of my Master. He criticized no one. For years I lived with that man, but never did I hear those lips utter one word of condemnation for any sect. He had the same sympathy for all sects; he had found the harmony between them. A man may be intellectual, or devotional, or mystic, or active, the various religions represent one or the other of these types. Yet it is possible to combine all the four in one man, and that is what future humanity is going to do. That was his idea. He condemned no one, but saw the good in all.

. . . As a fact, we all know that nothing will satisfy us until we know the truth for ourselves. However we may argue, however much we may hear, but one thing will satisfy us, and that is our own realization; and such an experience is possible for every one of us, if we will only try. The first ideal of this attempt to realize religion, is that of renunciation. As far as we can, we must give up . . . 'Ye cannot serve God and Mammon'. Let people try it if they will, and I have seen millions in every country who have tried; but after all, it comes to nothing. If one word remains true in the saying, it is, give up everything for the sake of the Lord. This is a hard and a long task, but you can begin it now. Bit by bit we must go towards it.

The second idea that I learnt from my Master, and which is perhaps the most vital, is the wonderful truth that the religions of the world are not contradictory or antagonistic. They are but various phases of one eternal religion. . . .

To learn this central secret that the truth may be one and yet many at the same time, that we may have different visions of the same truth from different standpoints, is exactly what must be done.

Then instead of antagonism to anyone, we shall have infinite sympathy with all. . . . Just as nature is unity in variety – an infinite variation in the phenomenal, that in and through all these variations of the phenomenal runs the Infinite, the Unchangeable, the Absolute Unity – so it is with every man; the microcosm is but a miniature repetition of the macrocosm; in spite of all these variations, in and through them all runs this eternal harmony, and we have to recognize this. . . .

That man was the embodiment of renunciation. . . . He was a

triumphant example, a living realization of the complete conquest of lust and of desire for money. He was beyond all ideas of either, and such men are necessary for this century. Such renunciation is necessary in these days when men have begun to think that they cannot live a month without what they call their 'necessities' and which they are increasing out of all proportion.

. . . The other idea of his life was intense love for others. The first part of my Master's life was spent in acquiring spirituality, and the remaining years in distributing it. . . . When the people heard that this holy man was likely to go from them soon, they began to come round him more than ever, and my Master went on teaching them without the least regard for his health. We could not prevent this. Many of the people came from long distances, and he would not rest until he had answered their question. 'While I can speak, I must teach them,' he would say, and he was as good as his word. . . .

My Master's message to mankind is : 'Be spiritual and realize truth for yourself.' He would have you give up selfishness for the sake of your fellow-beings. He would have you cease talking about love for your brother, and set to work to prove your words.

The time has come for renunciation, for realization; and then you will see the harmony in all the religions of the world. You will know that there is no need of any quarrel. And then only will you be ready to help humanity. To proclaim and make clear the fundamental unity underlying all religions was the mission of my Master. Other teachers have taught special religions which bear their names, but this great teacher of the nineteenth century made no claim for himself. He left every religion undisturbed because he had realized that, in reality, they are all part and parcel of the one eternal religion.

THE HARMONY IN LIFE

The harmony we have been considering, not only in the teachings but in the lives that lived out the teachings – as Vivekananda said, 'Anybody can *talk* !' – illustrates again and again the reconciliation of apparent opposites, both within each one of us, and in our relation to the world in which we live; and in the harmony between religions, sects and philosophies, between peoples, between individuals. Vivekananda said :

Coming from a country which is a hot-bed of religious sects, and to which, through its good fortune or ill-fortune, everyone who has a religious idea wants to send an advance-guard – I have been acquainted from my childhood with the various sects of the world.

He did not wish to be an advance-guard for yet one more sect. As he said of Ramakrishna, 'He left every religion undisturbed because he had realized that, in reality, they are part and parcel of the one eternal religion.' But he was determined to carry forward that great torrent of spirituality which flowed from Ramakrishna's life, which was hidden and yet open to all; composed equally of iron renunciation and childlike laughter, amusement and love to all who came; offering monasticism and yet completely open to those still living in the world and involved in it; clear-cut and uncompromising and yet gently taking each nature exactly where it stood, and helping it forward on its own natural path without any forcing. The Order which Vivekananda established must never trumpet its own name, never offer humanitarian service to the starving and the suffering in any spirit of conversion, but simply because all mankind is God incarnate, whom it is our privilege to serve; even our service is not our own, for, as Ramakrishna taught, it is a privilege to be the instrument of God, to be 'That' expressing Itself. In Ramakrishna's words :

It is God alone that he serves – God, who dwells in all beings . . . Helping others, doing good to others – this is the work of God alone . . .'

But what is God, and what is man, and wherein lies the relationship? As we have seen, Ramakrishna and Vivekananda spoke from experience, not from theory, and both were concerned with practical living in this world, and with the discovery of what *is*, not with providing an escape-route to unreality. What is real, they taught, is what is eternal; the inner Self of Man which is one with the whole Cosmic Consciousness, and That remains unchanging through many incarnations, witnessing the joys and sufferings of the soul as it moves in maya. Those who cannot believe in reincarnation, as Ramakrishna said to 'M', whose Western education made this belief difficult, will find that meditation and total trust will show them that this life is only a fraction of all that is, and the details of belief will depend on their own background; nobody must ever assert that his view, only, is the right one. No path is blocked. The path of the non-believer, who is sincerely seeking, lies open with all the others.

Let us look, once again, at the words of Vivekananda on the nature of Man, for they are crucial to all seekers.

Man is *not* bound by the law of causation. Pain and misery are not in Man, he is never born, he does not die, he is not in time and space. These ideas are mere reflections of the mind, but we mistake them for reality and so lose sight of the glorious truth they obscure. Time is but the method of our thinking, and we are the eternally present tense.'

The peace and strength which this brings may appear to be lost, again and again, as we struggle on, but, once glimpsed, we can never lose it, and the light will grow stronger with our resolution and determination. The swan searches for pools and ditches because she does not realize that she is already sailing on the lake; her 'flight to the lake beyond the mountains' means that she recognizes at last where she is, and always has been; the mountains are unreal, and of her own making. Vivekananda stressed that reality is here and now, whatever our nature may be.

He emphasized constantly, when speaking of bliss, that: 'We have not to *get* it; we have it. Let us wash away the dross from our eyes and see it. We must stand ever on the Self and look with perfect calmness upon all the panorama of the world.'

Which was all very well, as he said with his usual humour while he fought his tough battles and struggled through a life that contained much suffering and constant frustration: 'It is very easy

to talk! From my childhood I have heard of seeing God everywhere and in everything, and then I can really enjoy the world,
but as soon as I mix with the world, and get a few blows from it,
the idea vanishes. . . .'

And, as Ramakrishna said, it is all very well to go along, saying
'I am *That*' – up to the moment when a thorn pierces your foot.
Mere intellectual acceptance will not get us far, we may hear
the note of that great harmony, but we still have to learn to play
our own instrument. It is here that the worship of 'God with
form', 'God Personal' and possibly the worship of a great Incarnation, helps us, not as a spiritual therapy, or a psychological
bromide, but as a true expression of that Ultimate Reality.

'When we approach Him with the five senses,' said Vivekananda, in speaking of the impossibility of defining 'That' in
intellectual terms, for it is beyond words and can only be experienced, 'we can only see Him as the Personal God. The idea
is that the Self cannot be objectified. How can the knower know
Himself? But he can cast a shadow, as it were, and the highest
form of that shadow, that attempt as objectifying one's Self, is
the Personal God.'

And, of the Incarnation: 'Talk as you may, try as you may,
you cannot think of God but as a man. . . .' 'All these vessels go
to the sea of God to be filled, each according to its shape and
capacity. In man the water takes the shape of a man . . .'; and
his sardonic challenge to the man who despises the worship of an
Incarnation – 'ask him to define what he *means* by "omni-
science" ', and so on – it is through the great human vessel filled
to the brim with the 'water of God' that many people will come
to find that same Ultimate within themselves.

Ramakrishna gave his own experience.

God with form . . . like bubbles rising on a great expanse of water,
various divine forms are seen to rise out of the great Akasa of
Consciousness. The Incarnation of God is one of those forms. The
Primal Energy sports, as it were, through the activities of a divine
Incarnation. What is there in mere scholarship? God can be attained
by crying to Him, with a longing heart. . . .

And of personal God, called in Indian terms Ishwara, as the
soul is called Jiva: personal God is That Ultimate seen through
the mist of our senses; and as long as we are still bound within
the sense, said Vivekananda:

Jiva, the soul, and Ishwara, the personal God, are co-existent beings. As long as one exists, the other also must.

Vivekananda based his teachings and founded his Order on the acceptance of this great note in the harmony and also, as we have seen in the symbol he introduced, with the aim of encouraging each seeker to find and live out within himself the four great yogas, in varying proportions, and responding to them in the nature of others : Jnana, the Yoga of knowledge, the direct path of discrimination, leading to the Absolute; Bhakti, the joyful path of the positive, following love and devotion to a personal God; Karma Yoga, the Yoga of dedicated work, seen as a privilege and a service – God within man serving God in all others – and encircling them all, Raja Yoga, the Yoga of meditation, that daily practice in which 'the soul knows itself as it is – the unborn, the deathless, the birthless Being.'

All approaches, all paths are welcome. The Incarnation, or whatever form of God is worshipped by the seeker, is called the 'Chosen Ideal' and 'conversion' if it occurs, only exists in the sense of a natural attraction within the seeker, whether to Christ, to Buddha, to Krishna, to Ramakrishna himself; whoever it may be, this is chosen, not imposed. The most austere seekers of the Absolute are also welcomed by the Order and by the whole Ramakrishna movement; the man whose name it bears is obviously its heart and centre, and spirituality flows from the one who began it. And Ramakrishna himself, both austere and childlike, personal and withdrawn, 'full of fun and laughter' as was always said of him, yet with dignity and iron determination, was always approachable, but never a sentimentalist. He did not 'blur the edges'. To 'M', he once said :

Undoubtedly God exists in all beings as the All-pervading Spirit, but the manifestations of His power are different in different beings. In some places there is a greater manifestation of the power of Knowledge, in others, of the power of ignorance. Don't you see that among human beings there are cheats and gamblers, to say nothing of men who are like tigers. I think of them as the 'cheat God' the 'tiger God'.

'M' replied, smiling, by giving him back his own teaching : 'We should salute them from a distance. If we go near the "tiger God" and embrace him, he may devour us.'

There was a total lack of sentimentality in Ramakrishna's

experience of God; full of love and compassion as he was, he could not bear to see the coach-horses wearily dragging overladen carriages; still he taught, and taught firmly, that love, compassion and an acceptance of all that exists as expressions and manifestations of God, does not mean that we can associate closely with evil without being dangerously influenced by it; while we are living in this world of maya, if we eat hot food, our mouths are burned. The natural laws remain.

His love, joy and reverence towards the leaders and founders of other religions – even his dislike of regarding them as 'other', since his own spiritual experiences in samadhi had brought him to see that they were all manifestations of one great religion – caused him to insist all the more on a perfect following-out of one's own path. He used often the illustration of the Hindu daughter-in-law who lives in the house of her husband's family. She serves the other members of his family, she brings them water, she loves them all; but towards her husband, and to him only, she feels a special relationship. This refusal to blur the all-inclusive truth into eclectic vagueness was echoed by Vivekananda, who stressed often in his teachings in the West that Vedanta must always be clear-cut; nothing vague or indefinite.

The simile of water was often used by Ramakrishna; the great ocean of Brahman, moving into waves within maya; the great Incarnations or teachers as waves (or pieces of ice) which for a time assume a form which we can see and recognize, but which are in fact a part of that great Whole of which we too, though still partly in ignorance, are in truth also manifestations.

Madame Calvé, the great opera singer, expressed to Vivekananda her dislike of the idea of 'losing her individuality'. She did not want to be absorbed into an eternal unity. The word had no personal meaning for her; obviously, as a word, it sounded cold and abstract. Vivekananda again used the metaphor of water: the raindrop which falls into the ocean is rejoining *itself*. It is no longer separated, it is more fully itself than it could ever have been before, when it was one separate drop. And, referring to re-incarnation, he took the idea further. The raindrop could be drawn up again by the sun into the clouds. 'From there you can descend again, a little drop of water, a blessing and a benediction to the thirsty earth.'

On one occasion, 'M' asked Ramakrishna, 'Sir, what is the Spirit-form of God like?'

Ramakrishna reflected a moment, and then said softly, 'Shall I tell you what it is like? It is like water. One understands all this through spiritual discipline.'

His pause for reflection and the quietness of his reply may perhaps suggest that he was once more trying to express the inexpressible, as he always did when a sincere seeker asked a question for which there was no answer that he could yet fully understand until, after long practice, he gained the experience for himself. He immediately went on to give what seems almost contradictory advice; as always, he was resolving the paradox, showing clearly two sides of the coin. 'Water' may sound vague and formless to one who has not reached that stage; he gave a glimpse of it as near as words could convey, and then went on to advise 'M' to think of God with form, for, 'It is only after attaining Brahmanjnana that one sees non-duality, the oneness of Brahman and its Sakti.... When a man thinks of fire, he must also think of its power to burn. Again, when he thinks of the power to burn, he must also think of fire.'

The formless Absolute; God with form. All is He; all is That; but we are still in maya. Have many of us yet reached a state where we can honestly say we experience the full spiritual experience of the word 'love', without first thinking of a loving expression on somebody's face? If we see a loving act we think of the Ultimate Love of which it is an expression. We see the bubble, the wave, the ice – all with recognizable form – and we know that the whole ocean is there. Sometimes we may dive into the ocean, but we do not yet live in it constantly and consciously, at all times. Ramakrishna explained that some people have never heard of the ocean and do not believe it exists; others may have heard its sound from far off and may have met people who have swum in it. Others may approach its edge, others enter it by degrees, some can swim far out – and some, like a salt doll, enter it and at once become one with it.

His own experiences of the heights of the super-conscious interchanging constantly with warm humanity and also with practicality (he intensely disliked disorder or shoddiness in daily matters, or anything that was careless and thoughtless), constantly surprised those who fell at his feet because of his spiritual attainments, and then were surprised to find him (for example) giving practical help and advice to an old man whose son had just died, and who was overcome with grief.

When faced with this situation, as he often was, for death in India strikes frequently, it is noticeable that his approach to the grief-stricken parent was never at first an abstract one. He talked to him gently, and sometimes described how he, too, when he saw his young nephew die, rejoiced in spiritual ecstasy when he saw that the soul did not die with the body, but remained as it had always been; but next day, no longer in a high spiritual state, he faced a world from which someone had been removed, and for a time he felt, as he said, as though 'a wet cloth had been placed in his heart and wrung'. If he felt like that for the passing of a nephew, he said, how much worse must the suffering be for parents who lose a child? He never said 'I have reached the heights of the super-conscious in samadhi; I am beyond such things.'

To the grief-stricken, he always gave this advice for the time being, while grief remained: 'Death has entered the house – wrestle with it. Overcome it with the name of God!' This was a tonic, a bracing of oneself to meet human grief, not to be overwhelmed by it, but to fight, using the mantra as the sword, or as a life-line.

Lastly, and only then, he led on to a reminder of the great truth that God – in whatever form one experiences Him, or as the Absolute without form – 'That' remains as always; the tree is still there. One or two fruits may fall, but the tree remains. He gave the advice, too, that a lifetime's work of building strong ballast to the boat, in the way of daily meditation, prayer, the mantra, the constant thought of God like a light within the heart amidst daily duties – plus an occasional retreat from the world to gain spiritual strength and the company of 'holy men' (as those far along the path are called, in the East) – all this makes a ballast so that when the storm hits the boat, as it hits us all, we are rocked but we do not sink.

The harmony between our human life and the spiritual nature within us all was one which he constantly demonstrated. He approached each person who came to him, 'speaking in that person's language' as Vivekananda said, for each of us speaks a slightly different language, spiritually and psychologically. It is fascinating to see, in the great volume compiled by 'M' of Ramakrishna's discussions and talks with individuals who came to him, *The Gospel Of Sri Ramakrishna*, how the spiritual heights he had attained, had developed in him almost a spiritual radar system, so that he knew, as soon as someone approached him, what were the inner tendencies of that person, how far his or her spiritual potential could go, and in what direction; and many were helped and whole lives changed, simply by being with him.

On occasion, he even gave what appeared to be contradictory advice in matters of everyday behaviour; and then it became clear that he was dealing with totally different natures. In one case, he rebuked a young disciple who raged at some people who were criticizing Ramakrishna. The disciple used as his excuse that a disciple should defend his guru's good name at all times. Ramakrishna knew, however, that this young man had the spiritual weakness of possessing an aggressive nature and that he enjoyed being pugnacious. So he pointed out that nothing people said could hurt the guru, it was not the disciple's duty to practically overturn a boat on the Ganges simply because he was annoyed; he should speak quietly, or ignore the comments. Another disciple, however, was held back spiritually by excessive timidity which was in danger of becoming cowardice; in his case, Ramakrishna told him that when he heard criticism of his guru spoken, he should defend the guru verbally and stand up for what he believed. Either course of behaviour, taken to extreme, can obviously cause disharmony; what concerned Ramakrishna was the harmony within the nature of each disciple, and where there was a weakness, it had to be corrected.

It is of considerable importance that 'M' not only recounted what he saw and heard but gave helpful comment from his own knowledge of the person to whom Ramakrishna was speaking, so that the reader can sense the note of harmony in Ramakrishna's dealings with people. Without this, it would be all too easy to take one piece of advice given to one person, and turn it into almost a holy text which must be applied to all people and at all times. On the essentials he stood firm; on the applications of those essentials he spoke always to the individual, and the variety of individuals who visited him was enormous. We can never forget, as we read, that he had reached a state where he saw all people as manifestations of God, of 'That', and so as a part of himself; and his spiritual knowledge of them, including occasions when they were not with him, can be seen growing and deepening, especially as he approached his own death. On more than one occasion he foresaw the approaching – and quite unexpected – death of a disciple, and so changed his usual advice to those 'in the world'. The advice to work out to the full their duties and then offer the fruits to God, and not to wrench themselves into renunciation before they were spiritually ready for it – if death was approaching, he changed this into advice, almost into a definite instruction – to put aside all worldly duties and turn completely to God. For instance, a close and devoted disciple of Ramakrishna called Adhar, came to him one day when 'M' was in the room with him. Adhar explained that he had been unable to visit him for a few days because he had been very busy attending a conference of his school committee and various other meetings. After a time, says 'M', Ramakrishna suddenly said to Adhar, 'Look here. All these are unreal – meetings, school, office and everything else. God alone is the substance, and all else is illusory. One should worship God with one's whole mind. . . . This moment the body is, and the next moment it is not. One must make haste to worship God.'

Adhar sat without speaking a word. After a while, he said humbly, 'Sir, you haven't been to our place for a long time. The drawing-room smells worldly and everything else appears to be steeped in darkness.'

'M' continues, in his account :

The Master was deeply touched by these words of his devotee – He suddenly stood up and blessed 'M' and Adhar in ecstatic mood, touching their heads and hearts. In a voice choked with love, the Master said : 'I look upon you as Narayana [God] Himself. You are indeed my own.'

And in a footnote 'M' adds one comment : 'A few months after this conversation, Adhar died.'

There are many conversations throughout 'M' 's *Gospel Of Sri Ramakrishna*; he was a faithful and accurate recorder, and in his extreme humility, he kept himself very much out of the picture. When Vivekananda first read his account, some years after the death of Ramakrishna, he was full of praise for the accuracy and truth to life of the record 'M' was compiling in what is now *The Gospel Of Sri Ramakrishna*. In a letter to him, Vivekananda wrote, 'Never was the life of a great Teacher brought before the public untarnished by the writer's mind, as you are presenting this one. . . . The Socratic dialogues are Plato all over; you are entirely hidden. Moreover the dramatic part is infinitely beautiful.'

Ramakrishna made no sect, established no new creed or dogma;

it is not possible to say 'I am a Ramakrishna-ite' or 'This, in a few brief phrases, is what he taught'. He established a harmony, both within the warring aspects of man's nature and between religions, creeds, philosophies and sects; he made no claims for himself whatever, and he gave no public lectures. But the accounts of those who knew him; the speaking, writing and the building of compassionate humanitarian work which Vivekananda caused to flow across the world in an ever-growing flood, never lost touch with the transcendent and with the greatness in man, and it never lost its humanity and simplicity. It 'spoke to each man in his own language' and it placed the greatest emphasis of all on the development of spirituality.

As Ramakrishna said, it is useless to offer religion to a man starving to death. But when he is fed he may still be unhappy; practical service is a part of our life; we must be joyful to be the instruments of God; it is God in us, helping God in others. But there is a higher duty still; the spiritual is highest of all.

Vivekananda said of him :

His first principle was – first, form character, first earn spirituality, and results will come of themselves. His favourite illustration was, 'When the lotus opens, the bees come of their own accord to seek the honey; so let the lotus of your character be full blown, and the results will follow.'

Forming character, earning spirituality; this was to be done by the development and harmonizing of the four yogas within us, as we have seen, and by the harmonizing and using of the three gunas – even the lowest and darkest part of our characters can thus be *used*, to help lift us towards sattva, the highest guna. So we shall move also to a harmony between ourselves, between our own religion and philosophy, and all others.

The pitfalls in the way were emphasized over and over again. Egotism. Bigotry. And all forms of materialism which tie us to the body, especially lust, and love of money, and power. All forms of greed : everything which makes us feel 'I am the body' or 'I am the brain' or 'I am this personality'. For in every one of these lurks a weakness, a fear of loss. This subconsciously increases nervous tension and the inevitability of frustration and disappointment.

. . . The soul of man is like a piece of crystal, but it takes the colour of whatever is near it. That is the difficulty. That constitutes the bondage. We have taken the 'colour' of the body and have forgotten what we are. The crystal which reflects the colour red, thinks it is red. All our fears, all worries, anxieties, troubles, mistakes, weakness, evil, are from that great blunder, that we think we are bodies . . . the practice of meditation is pursued. The crystal knows what it is, takes its own colour.

And, again, 'Excepting the infinite spirit, everything is changing. There is the whirl of change. Permanence is nowhere except in yourself. *There* is the infinite joy, unchanging.'

Even those powers which the West calls 'psychic' or 'occult' were regarded by Ramakrishna as possible stumbling stones on the path, and Vivekananda constantly warned his disciples to avoid any excitement over, or involvement with, anything which he described as 'uncanny'. Both Ramakrishna and Vivekananda themselves showed on various occasions powers which in the West would be regarded as miraculous, though in Vedanta they would be regarded as simply manifestations of natural spiritual laws, which occurred when certain spiritual heights were reached – and sometimes at a lower stage, in some degree – but to take them seriously led to dangers or even ruin, deflecting the seeker from the true path of spirituality and character-forming. Ramakrishna often prayed that the great 'psychic powers' should be kept from him, as they would hold him back, and those manifestations in him which we would regard as miraculous or 'psychic' he did not advertise, and regarded as unimportant. Crowds would come to see the miraculous, where they would not cross the street to see pure goodness or the heights of spirituality, as Jesus also said. And within the aspirant himself, a fascination with any psychic powers he might develop, could be very dangerous, and lead away from the heights. In any case, said Vivekananda, they come and go. It is even possible for a seeker who is proceeding swiftly towards spiritual heights, to worry because he has developed no 'psychic powers'. Such things, they both taught, certainly exist, but they are not important; they may even be a danger to spiritual development.

What, then, *are* the first signs? That streak of dawn across the sky, as Ramakrishna said, which shows that the sun will soon rise, and that daylight is coming?

It is, at first, a negation. In his own homely words, it is the child who has previously been quite contentedly playing with toys, who realizes that a lifetime with toys is not enough; the child will have no more to do with toys, he cries for mother, and will not be satisfied. 'And to him alone, the Mother comes running'. The disillusionment with toys may come slowly, or it may be sudden; but for a time there is a turning away; a negation of what previously was all-important; a restlessness; a longing. That longing, said Ramakrishna, is the vital sign, the first streak of light in the morning sky.

Then for a time we live as aliens in this strange world, this universe of maya, in part belonging to it, like the servant girl who is partially at home in her master's house, and yet knows that her true home is in her native village. She continues to perform her duties, she may even be content in her present house and calls it 'home', but in her heart, she knows that it is not. She is only there for a while.

Then, at last, comes the realization that 'All is That', 'All is He', 'In all things shines the Face of Faces'. The seeker, even before he realizes ultimate Union, and while there may be still some degree of separation, now walks in a world in which only two people exist; himself and his God, and everything and everybody is a manifestation of Him. Or, if he is a jnani, of his own great Self. However often he may slip back, once he has seen this, the sun has really begun to rise. To quote Vivekananda :

Every moment, really, we are enjoying the absolute bliss, though covered-up, misunderstood, and caricatured. . . . But to understand that, we have to go through the negation, and then the positive side will begin. We have to give up ignorance and all that is false, and then truth will begin to reveal itself to us. When we have grasped the truth, things which we gave up at first, will take new shape and form, will appear to us in a new light, and become deified. They will have become sublimated, and then we shall understand them in their true light . . . we must give them up first, and then we get them back again, deified.

This, he emphasized, was the meaning of 'renunciation' – deification. Renunciation was Ramakrishna's great jewel. And why worry about failures ! By failures we learn, said Vivekananda, they are beautiful, these failures. We get up and go on. For we are not isolated, a 'separate mud-puddle' – we are a part of that infinite ocean of Blessedness; in the words which have been regarded as sacred, in the Katha Upanishad, for untold centuries :

There are two selves, the apparent Self and the real Self. Of these it is the real Self, and he alone, who must be felt as truly existing. To the man who has felt him as truly existing, he reveals his inmost nature. . . . He shining, everything shines.

The great notes of the harmony remain the same; there is no compromise, no weakness, no vagueness. But the tune is capable of infinite variety; 'unity in diversity'; and it is continually changing, developing; never static. Music is always moving. In the words of Ramakrishna, 'As long as I live, I learn.' And Vivekananda :

We admit the imperfection of our system, because the reality must be beyond all systems; and in this admission lies the promise and portent of an eternal growth. Sects, ceremonies, and books, so far as they are the means of a man's realizing his own nature, are all right. When he has realized *that*, he gives up everything.

The reconciliation of opposites; the final realization that apparent paradoxes in spiritual life may in fact be two sides of the same coin. They are ultimately reconciled and resolved within each one of us; as Vivekananda said, in the end nothing will satisfy us but our own experience. And in our relationship with others, it is what we are, rather than what we say, that matters.

Ramakrishna and Vivekananda were their own best illustration. The enormous spiritual strength and energy of Vivekananda, combined always with the childlike frankness and open laughter which drew people to him, sometimes in crowds of thousands, and also as individuals, always showed the two sides of the coin; and however exhausted he became by life's battles, he came always to the place where the questioner stood in his own spiritual path, and for the moment forgot all others. He spoke to each man in his own language.

His Master, Ramakrishna, had brought this to even greater heights; and in him were constantly shown the renunciation and great teaching, as well as the frequent heights of samadhi, side by side with a sudden plunge into mimicry and acting to make the youngsters laugh. On one occasion, one of them laughed so much that he fell down, and Ramakrishna, who could be a strict perfectionist on occasion, simply said joyfully, 'Look at that child ! He is rolling with laughter !'

His great disciple, Ramakrishnananda, who was with him as a young man and helped to nurse him throughout his long and slow dying, and was nursing him as he died, spoke about him to an

American devotee of the Ramakrishna Vedanta Society in New York. She had been introduced to Vedanta by Vivekananda himself. Ramakrishnananda said to her, describing Ramakrishna :

Although he was very gentle, sometimes he would be so awe-inspiring that even one word from him would make you tremble. . . . Yet if one of his own made a mistake, nearly always he would check him in the gentlest, most loving manner, just as a loving father would his own son.

And that great resolution of apparent opposites – 'softer than flowers, stronger than adamant', which is the essence of harmony, for only a sentimentalist continually plays one monotonous theme :

Every time you went to see him you felt as if a great load had been taken off your back and off your mind. Whatever doubt you had in your mind was sure to be cleared, without putting any question. Yet he was always simple and humble in his manner towards everyone and ready to learn even from a baby.

There can be no summing-up of a harmony; like all music, it grows, it moves. But perhaps the notes which linger most often in the minds of those who find much insecurity and anxiety in this chaotic world, are those which lead to the turning away from 'making-do' with pools and ditches, and, like Kabir's swan, finding our true home in the lake. But Ramakrishna taught, and Vivekananda insisted in every word he spoke, we can only come home in ways which are practical, which are not vaguely theoretical, which are true to our own very varying natures, and do no violence to the natures of others.

Ramakrishna knew and loved the great truths of the Upanishads and the Gita, of the Hindu religious epics and the poetry of Kabir, the fifteenth century mystical poet and religious leader who combined in himself the traits of Muslim and Hindu; Ramakrishna often quoted the saying of Kabir, 'The Formless Absolute is my Father, and God with Form is my Mother'. But he set them all aside to seek and experience truth for himself. If was only after he had experienced, that he found in them all, fully, that same truth, and again he found truth in other religions, and the recognition delighted him because it expressed his own experience. His insistence on absolute sincerity led him to teach that renunciation (that word so much feared in the West, a word defined by Vivekananda as 'deification') flowers naturally through different stages, it is not forced or arid. For those involved in the world and its duties, the renunciation may be mental rather than actual, but it will lead to a point when we find that pools and ditches are not enough, we feel 'alien' in the best and truest sense; we are beginning to find our true home, and so we become willing but only partly involved aliens in this world of maya. In his own words, 'The wise ant takes the grains of sugar and leaves the grains of sand.'

And then comes the supreme note of harmony, the note which completes the chord. We have said 'no' and now, totally, we can say yes; we have given up on one level, only to receive again, on another level, all things deified. In the words of the Upanishads, 'He shining, everything shines.' What we have found in ourselves, we find everywhere. Says the Isha Upanishad :

In the heart of all things, of whatever there is in the universe, dwells the Lord. He alone is the reality . . . To the illumined soul, the Self is all. For him who sees everywhere oneness, how can there be delusion or grief?

In the dying words of Sarada Devi,

Learn to make the whole world your own. No one is a stranger, my child; this whole world is your own.

She was echoing the words of Ramakrishna :

One must love all. No one is a stranger. It is Hari who exists in all beings. Nothing exists without him.'

In that sense, and in that sense only, alienation cannot exist and disharmony and chaos are forgotten, as darkness is forgotten in the light of the morning. After many struggles the swan sails at last on the lake beyond the mountains and knows that the mountains were self-created; whatever the nature of the seeker, It knows Itself and so It knows all else.

No one is a stranger.

GLOSSARY

ADVAITA VEDANTA   doctrine of the oneness of God, soul, and universe; this One is called Brahman, Atman, the Ultimate, or Satchidananda (Existence-Knowledge-Bliss Absolute). Non-dual but including various stages of Dualism in approach. Ramakrishna likened Brahman to an infinite ocean in which Personal God, and Incarnations of God, are pieces of ice with recognizable form, and so are aspects of the same 'ocean'. But the 'ocean' itself is ultimately non-dual.

APRATIKULYA   belief that nothing that happens to us is really against us.

ASANA   *see* PATANJALI.

ATMAN   the Individual Soul, which, in the doctrine of the Advaita Vedanta, is one with the Supreme Soul.

AVIDYA   *see* MAYA.

BHAGAVAD-GITA   'The Song Of God.' The most well-known scripture of Hinduism. A portion of the epic *Mahabharata.*

BHAKTA   one who follows the path of Bhakti.

BHAKTI YOGA   the yoga of devotion and love to a personal God, to one's 'Chosen Ideal'.

BHAVA   many meanings, but here used specifically to denote one of the five relationships which a dualistic worshipper assumes towards God. The relationships, or attitudes, are, Shanta (Santa) : the serene, peaceful attitude of a devotee. Dasya : the attitude of servant to master. Sakhya : the attitude of friend to friend. Vatsalya : the attitude of parent to child. Madhura : the attitude of lover to lover, or husband to wife.

BRAHMAN   the Absolute; the Ultimate Reality of the Vedanta philosophy.

BRAHMIN   the highest caste in the Hindu caste system.

BRAHMO SAMAJ   a monotheistic society founded by Raja Rammohan Roy.

DASYA   *see* BHAVA.

DHARANA   *see* PATANJALI.

DHYANA *see* PATANJALI.

DUALISM   belief that the soul and Personal God are (in varying degrees) distinct and separate from each other.

GUNAS   the three gunas, sattva, rajas, and tamas, are regarded as the essence of maya; everything consists of these three, throughout the universe. Guna also means a strand or rope, so, figuratively, the gunas bind souls to transmigration. Sattva, the highest, is manifested as equilibrium, serenity, compassion, detachment, and all the nobler qualities; rajas manifests as energy, activity, involvement, restlessness, and sometimes pride and egotism; tamas as inertia, darkness, brutality, and the lowest qualities. The gunas are constantly changing.

GURU   spiritual teacher, who initiates the disciple with the mantra.

HATHA YOGA   The yoga of bodily control.

HATHA YOGI   one following path of the Hatha Yoga.

ISHTA   the Chosen Ideal; a form of God chosen by the spiritual aspirant, on which his devotion and meditation centres; an Incarnation, God, or Principle.

ISHWARA (ISHVARA)   personal God; God with attributes.

JIVA   the embodied soul; a living being. Philosophically, Brahman manifesting in maya; but the Jiva, in ignorance, imagines itself as separate and sees the One as many.

JNANA YOGA   the yoga of knowledge, philosophy, and discrimination between the real and the unreal; ultimately it is non-dual.

JNANI   a jnana yogi; one who follows the path of Jnana Yoga.

KALI   the deity of the Dakshineswar Kali temple, worshipped by Ramakrishna as God the Mother; the Adyasakti, the Primal Energy; the power of Brahman, who has become the three gunas, and who creates and preserves, also destroys, the universe; she is regarded as symbolizing maya, and so as the Mother who finally leads the soul to union with Brahman, in realization, when the soul loses the illusion of separation.

KARMA   action.

KARMA YOGA   the yoga of selfless action; work performed without attachment to the resuts of work, in which the fruits of action are dedicated to God. (Also can refer to ritualistic worship.)

KARMA YOGI   one who follows the path of Karma Yoga.

KRISHNA   an incarnation of God, one of the Ideal Deities of the Vaishnavas. The Bhagavad-Gita consists mainly of Krishna's teachings to Arjuna, who was his friend and disciple.

KUNDALINI   spiritual energy which passes upwards from the base of the spine to the cerebrum in the highest stages of meditation.

MADHURA   *see* BHAVA.

MANTRA(M)   sacred formula used in repetition (Japam), in meditation and throughout the day; it is regarded as possessing great protective and strengthening power; a loving and concentrated repetition of it draws the mind to the Chosen Ideal and to the Ultimate; it usually includes the name of the aspirant's Chosen Ideal.

MAYA   the Cosmic Illusion, in which the One appears as many, the Absolute appears as relative. Brahman is the Being, Maya the Becoming (see Kali). Avidyamaya: the aspect of maya which entangles the soul further (anger, passion, hatred and so on); Vidyamaya consists of the nobler qualities, actions and circumstances, which lead to eventual liberation.

NARAYANA   a name of God; in particular, a name of Vishnu.

NIRVIKALPA SAMADHI   *see* SAMADHI.

NIYAMA   *see* PATANJALI.

NON-DUALISM   monism. *See* ADVAITA VEDANTA.

OJAS   energy conveyed by the nerve-currents, including sex-energy, which is used in meditation.

OM (AUM)   the most sacred word of the Vedas; a symbol of Brahman and of God in all aspects; all other mantras are derived from it and it includes them all.

PARAMAHAMSA   one who has attained a high level of spiritual illumination.

PATANJALI   great teacher of yoga aphorisms, on whose teachings the eight steps of meditation are based. These steps are, Yama: ethical living. Niyama: cleanliness of body and mind, devotion to God. Asana: posture for meditation. Pranayama: control of the Prana (vital energy) which may include breath control. Pratyahara: gathering-in of the scattered forces of the mind. Dharana: fixing the mind on one spot (the object of meditattion). Dhyana: the mind flowing directly, without a break, continually towards the object of meditation. Samadhi: the super-conscious state; ecstasy; trance-state. *See* SAMADHI for two types of Samadhi.

PRANAYAMA   *see* PATANJALI.

PRATYAHARA　*see* PATANJALI.

QUALIFIED NON-DUALISM　a school of Vedanta founded by Ramanuja, in which the individual soul is regarded as part of God,
not wholly separate. He also emphasized love and faith in God.

RADHA　Krishna's closest companion among the gopis of Vrin-
davan. Symbolizes the attraction between the soul and God.

RAJA YOGA　the yoga of meditation; the concentrated control of
man's inner nature.

RAJA YOGI　one following the path of Raja Yoga.

RAJAS　*see* GUNAS.

SADHU　a monk.

SAKHYA　*see* BHAVA.

SAKTI (SHAKTI)　a name of God worshipped as mother (*see* KALI);
the creative power of Brahman. Sometimes used simply to mean
a woman.

SAMADHI　the super-conscious state; ecstasy; communion with
God. In Savikalpa Samadhi (Bhavasamadhi), the distinction
between the soul and God is still maintained. Nirvikalpa
Samadhi, is the highest state of Samadhi, in which the aspirant
realizes in full experience his complete oneness with Brahman.

SANNYASIN　a monk.

SANNYASINI　a nun.

SATCHIDANANDA　Existence-Knowledge-Bliss Absolute. A name
of Brahman, the ultimate Reality.

SATTVA　*see* GUNAS.

SHANTA (SANTA)　*see* BHAVA.

SIVA (SHIVA)　great and auspicious god of Hinduism. Also the
Dissolver aspect of godhead, when seen as creator, preserver
and dissolver.

SUSHUMNA　hollow canal within the spinal column, extending
from the base of the spine to the brain, up which the awakened
spiritual energy arises. *See* KUNDALINI.

SWAMI　title of respect given to a monk.

TAMAS　*see* GUNAS.

UPANISHADS　second part of the Vedas, the oldest and most
important of the Hindu scriptures; it is especially concerned
with the Knowledge of God (Jnana) and all aspects of religious
truth leading to ultimate Realization of Brahman.

VATSALYA　*see* BHAVAS.

VEDANTA　*see* UPANISHADS. The word 'Vedanta' was used by
Vivekananda in preference to 'Hinduism', to convey all schools

of thought and religion leading to ultimate Union; the essence of the Vedas.

VEDAS the oldest and most important of the Hindu scriptures.

VIDYA (VIDYAMAYA) *see* MAYA.

YAMA *see* PATANJALI.

YOGA word meaning yoke or union; the conscious union of the individual soul and the Universal Soul; also the method by which to realize this union.

YOGI One who practises yoga; may also refer to one who has achieved Union.

BIBLIOGRAPHY

'M' (Mahendranath Gupta) *The Gospel Of Sri Ramakrishna*, translated by Swami Nikhilananda: Ramakrishna Vedanta Centre, New York.

Swami Saradananda, *Sri Ramakrishna The Great Master*: Sri Ramakrishna Math, Madras.

The Message Of Our Master, by some of the direct disciples of Ramakrishna: Advaita Ashrama, Calcutta.

Swami Ghanananda, *Sri Ramakrishna, His Unique Message*: Ramakrishna Vedanta Centre, UK.

Swami Vivekananda, *Complete Works*, vols 1–8 (including his letters): Advaita Ashrama, Calcutta.

Life of Swami Vivekananda, by his Eastern and Western disciples and friends: Advaita Ashrama, Calcutta.

Reminiscences of Swami Vivekananda, by Eastern and Western friends: Advaita Ashrama, Calcutta.

Swami Vivekananda In East And West, collection of essays by various authors: Ramakrishna Vedanta Centre, UK.

Sister Nivedita, *The Master As I Saw Him*: Udbodham Office, Calcutta.

Swami Nikhilananda, *Holy Mother* (Sri Sarada Devi): Ramakrishna-Vivekananda Centre, New York.

Swami Tapasyananda and Swami Nikhilananda, *Sri Sarada Devi* (Life and conversations): Sri Ramakrishna Math, Madras.

Many books about or by the direct disciples of Ramakrishna, including :

The Apostles of Ramakrishna, compiled by Swami Gambhirananda : Advaita Ashrama, Calcutta.

Swami Shivananda, *For Seekers Of God* : Advaita Ashrama, Calcutta.

The Eternal Companion (accounts and teachings of Swami Brahmananda) : Sri Ramakrishna Math, Madras.

Swami Virajananda, *Paramartha Prasanga* ('Towards The Goal Supreme') : Advaita Ashrama, Calcutta.

Swami Premananda, *Teachings and Reminiscences* : Vedanta Press, Hollywood, Calif. US.

Sister Devamata, *Days in an Indian Monastery* : The Vedanta Centre, Chasset, Mass. and Ananda Ashrama, La Crescenta, Calif.' US.

The teachings of Swami Vivekananda on the four yogas are published separately, as individual books.

The books listed here are all contemporary and first-hand accounts, by or about the people concerned, and their teachings. These books (and information) are obtainable in UK from the Ramakrishna Vedanta Centre, Bourne End, Bucks.